THE MOMENTUM EFFECT

Pushing Your Boundaries to Harness the Power of Success

KEVIN E. FRANCE

Former Fortune 50 Divisional Sales Director
Founder of Momentum Consulting Group Inc. & i-Consulting Group

Copyright © Kevin France 2018

All rights reserved. No part of this publication may be reproduced, stored in a retrieval system, or transmitted in any form or by any means—electronic, mechanical, photocopying, recording or otherwise—without prior written permission from the publisher.

Contact: www.info@MomentumConsultingGrp.com
Website: www.MomentumConsultingGrp.com

What People Say About *The Momentum Effect*

"Navigating the corporate jungle just got easier after reading *The Momentum Effect.* Drawing from his own personal experiences and 'key learnings', Kevin France effectively shows us how to spot emerging opportunities by focusing on what matters most or, as he puts it, 'fishing where the fish are.' Real-world case studies between the chapters make each principle both personal and relevant."

Stephen M. R. Covey, *New York Times* bestselling author of *The Speed of Trust* and co-author of *Smart Trust;* Co-founder and Global Practice Leader, Franklin Covey's Global Speed of Trust Practice

"*The Momentum Effect* has some great nuggets of wisdom for any budding entrepreneur to learn from—pay particular attention to the learning points at the end of each chapter"

Hugh G. Hilton, J.D., Chief Executive Officer, Alvarez & Marsal Capital Real Estate, LLC

"Insert Kevin into your life or business, he has great ideas and the mindset for success."

Wayne Allyn Root, Former U.S. Vice Presidential nominee, and Bestselling Business Author, "The Power of RELENTLESS

"*The Momentum Effect* provides a compass on how to be successful in building company health, growth, and profitability. It promotes the tenets of simplicity, innovation, and stretching one's comfort zone while maintaining balance in your personal life. Kevin France provides the reader with an insight into what made him a success and how he always put his customers first. I should know, I was one!"

Dale L. Wright, Divisional former President, and COO, Amerinet, Inc.

"This is a must read for every sales team. The author combines a sense of vision for what is possible in every type of sales position with much to-the-point guidance for understanding how to transform poor sales performance into market-leading results.

Each chapter includes case studies and ends with cogent tips as key takeaways. This is a book sales people should keep handy as a guide and source of inspiration during those long slogs when success seems far removed. The author reminds us that success may be just around the corner."

Mark Heuer, PhD, Associate Professor, Management Sigmund Weis School of Business

FOREWORD

In *The Momentum Effect*, Kevin France takes us on a breathtaking, roller-coaster ride through the earlier part of his career. Using the breadth of his experiences to highlight a host of critical learning points about improving business performance, it's all backed up with case studies from his advisory work.

Telling of numerous improvement initiatives that he has implemented across the years, both the title of Kevin's book and his present-day consulting practice accurately describe how he approaches his work in driving change and turning businesses around: it's all about creating *momentum.*

I thoroughly enjoyed this book, a non-fiction thriller jam-packed with entirely practical and wholly actionable business improvement strategies that can be adapted to a multitude of situations.

Any business leader, student of business or aspiring entrepreneur can learn from Kevin's vignettes in *The Momentum Effect*, and I have every confidence that all who read this book will find it to be both highly rewarding and truly inspirational.

Dr. Wayne Ruga
Entrepreneur, innovator, architect, and scholar
Loeb Fellow, Harvard Graduate School of Design
West Kirby, England, June 2018
www.thecaritasproject.info

This book is dedicated to my wife Deborah, who has always been a source of true inspiration and has unfailingly encouraged me through the toughest of times. I probably—perhaps certainly—would not have written this book without her constant uplifting spirit and love that got the project started and helped bring it to fruition.

Deborah my love, I thank you for being my compass and beacon to guide me through adversity and for your faith and belief in me, no matter what ventures I take on. This book is as much yours as it is mine, and for that, I will be eternally grateful.

Contents

INTRODUCTION

IT'S A RATHER disturbing fact that after just seven years of operation, 63% of businesses fail. A quarter of these never make it past the first year, and 44% are closed by the end of year three. There are numerous reasons for these sad statistics, but factors like inadequate planning, lack of business experience, not having differential in the marketplace, limited market awareness, and an unclear focus all contribute significantly to their failure.

With the right help and guidance, many of these pitfalls may be avoided, and that's why I wrote this book. I have the knowledge and experience to help businesses thrive and more importantly, because I care, I want to help you build and fortify your enterprise. This is a story of how my career brought me significant success, and I want to share with you what I've learned along the way.

Starting off as the average employee who discovered his own creativity and aptitude for business and leadership, I understood that becoming successful takes a *lot* of effort as well. I didn't just sit back and watch the dollars roll in, and many people who know me would put me in the 'workaholic' category.

Whatever your circumstances, you must correctly evaluate the opportunities that will propel you forward, and then seize them with gusto. You need to form and nurture mutually beneficial relationships that align with your direction and goals.

Being cognizant of key areas where personal growth was required helped me stay focused on what I wanted to achieve from a business perspective. One highly successful businessman, a friend who mentored me, noted that I never stopped working on improving myself.

There were always new opportunities and new methods for accomplishing more in the best possible way. The old adage that "success breeds success" is very true if you truly want to make it happen. You have to create that initial momentum yourself and keep building on it. You have to keep pushing your boundaries and never give up.

My story is a testament to how my theories have worked for me, and how they can also work for you. Over the years, I've compiled the lessons, tips, and guidance that came my way to help you identify and address areas of improvement and foster your strengths, so you can develop your own momentum effect.

It took me nearly 30 years of employment to realize that I was better off doing what I love on a full-time basis. Since that epiphany moment, I've set up two consulting companies with the intention of helping other businesses grow. After numerous successes with my clients, which proved I could make a real difference, I decided to write this book to demonstrate that my ideas in action are far more effective than mere discussions on unproven theories.

Cut-and-dried business theories have their place, but for me, real-life success stories are easier to relate to and more inspiring. It becomes personal because you realize that if the average employee can achieve truly significant career success like I did, then you can also do it. Sharing my experiences allows me to impart my insights on the essentials of success, which you can also apply in your enterprise.

In this book, I have cited several recognizable and practical learning points, all of which are summarized at the end of each chapter. You will also encounter my case studies, relevant to their respective chapter's theme, so you can see how I've applied what I've learned. No matter what rung you're on in the corporate or entrepreneurial ladder, this book has something useful for you.

My story is my gift to you. It is a testament to the fact that there are several paths to success, and by creating momentum through belief, focus, persistence, and the right mindset, you can find yours.

To your success,

Kevin E. France

1

Never Fail To Grasp An Opportunity

"You have to believe in yourself before anybody else believes in you."

Ray LaMontagne

IT'S BEEN A roller-coaster journey to get where I am today, but rather than starting right at the beginning of my career, let me begin with my bravest decision. The title of this first chapter has to be some of the best advice I can give, so let's start from when I left my role with a cookie company.

The upside was that I was appointed as the National Accounts Manager of a major product supply and distribution corporation, whose annual sales at that time were about $1.8 billion. The downside was that I took a $70,000 a year pay cut!

My previous company had taken good care of me, but there was no potential for any further personal growth. With my new employer, the opportunities were huge, and my only desire was to keep moving onward and upward. Therefore, what I saw as a *temporary* reduction in pay was far outweighed by the expected long-term benefits. I knew that *real* success was within reach, and now I certainly had the drive to achieve it!

Upon leaving the cookie company, they wished me luck and said they could see I needed to get on a better, more aggressive and, they admitted, more progressive career path to broaden my experience. I was always taught never to burn bridges and was glad to depart on a positive note.

My new primary goals were to develop and strengthen existing national customer relationships by encouraging them to buy more, and to further increase my sales revenue by bringing in new national accounts. I was now exposed to a far more sophisticated buyer than previously, dealing with corporations of significant size and stature. Most were at least Fortune 500 companies and in a lot of cases, Fortune 100.

My sales approach and business acumen certainly had to be elevated; it was such a different mentality from the grocery industry. Meeting with much more senior people required me to step up my game accordingly. All of my skills, including how I interacted with people, had to be polished even further. After all, I was now dealing with bigger clients, all highly seasoned professionals.

I was based out of the new Dallas Distribution Center, which had about a million square feet of office and warehouse space. There were also more than thirty other locations across the country. My responsibilities included handling all the national accounts, with the likes of major airlines, banks, and technology companies. My boss, the director of national accounts, was also based in Dallas.

My new company was known for its expertise in TQM (Total Quality Management). With a 'buttoned down' and process-driven culture, this was radically different from the environment I had just come from.

I was also introduced to Activity-Based Costing (ABC), which my new employers developed so precisely they could tell you exactly how much it cost for a person to walk different distances across a warehouse to pick a product for a customer. Managing the biggest airline account was my first exposure to ABC.

From a relationship management perspective, I was handed this piece of business to build and nurture. Executive management, however, was looking at the profitability. They understood that this was a 'flagship account', but nonetheless, they wanted it to be as profitable as possible.

We sold the airline almost everything it could use, from drinking cups to in-flight children's coloring books, as well as the wheel chocks that held the planes in place at the gate. We were so heavily into the mission-critical commodity business that if, for example, the plane did not have drinking cups, then it couldn't take off. In fact, we could have brought the company to a halt if we did not complete our part of the supply chain effectively and reliably. Thus, we had to ensure that this was a non-event!

Early into my post, I was brought into the CEO's office for a discussion on why we couldn't get the account to be more profitable. Upon investigation, it turned out that the drinking cups were the single largest item our client bought, but the margin was so small we practically weren't profiting from it. It dawned on me then that they hadn't considered the ABC numbers.

The airline placed orders every three weeks, and each of these meant about five minutes of interaction on behalf of our staff. The client called in or faxed their orders (email and the Internet were just starting up at that time), which were entered into the system. Then we simply waited until the requested items were picked up from the warehouse.

I started looking at the numbers differently, taking into account the cost of associating with the customer, which ultimately revealed a gross profit of about $30,000 for each order that only required five minutes of work! That was just one aspect of business done, so our ABC Team back at headquarters went headlong into a full review of the account to see what else we could uncover. When my boss and the CEO reviewed my findings, they realized this was actually an immensely profitable account!

This level of detail can give you a very different view from a broad perspective. At one point, the company executives were considering letting go of the account, but an alternative view on a different set of numbers completely changed their minds.

Once I settled into the company's system and was comfortable with my new sales approaches, my prior experience meant that building the business became second nature. I even picked up a couple of accounts that had a combined worth of around $8 million. This was not unusual in this company, as we had the largest and best national accounts division out of all of our competitors.

Despite my successes, after twelve months I was considering moving on since I still saw this position as a stepping-stone towards a better one. But my boss called me into his office and asked if I was interested in 'filling in' as the National Account Manager watching over the healthcare division.

Even though I wouldn't be officially appointed, this was an opportunity that couldn't be missed. With confidence that I could make this another sure success, and knowing it would certainly elevate my standing within the company, I readily accepted. A year later, I didn't get the job officially; I went one better and was promoted to the Healthcare Division as Director.

The Director of National Accounts realized that I eagerly faced challenges head-on. In broad terms, he wanted me to grow the company from its present $82M per year and number three position in the industry but didn't give me any immediate or more specific targets as he understood that I would set my own. With that opportunity in my hands, our number one competitor became my main target.

That night, I told my wife that my salary was now on its way back to its previous level, and after dinner, I wrote myself some goals. I focused on a SWOT Analysis (Strengths, Weakness, Opportunities, and Threats) and to this day, the points I noted are still crystal-clear in my memory:

1. Understand the healthcare market and the dynamics that are in play.
2. Know our strengths and where we are most vulnerable.
3. Mobilize our selling effort to maximize its effectiveness.
4. Create market awareness so I can start to develop end-user credibility.
5. Address employee education and grow our other 'information resources' on the basis that information is power and power = empowerment = sales.
6. Diversify our product offering because customers like choices, value relationships, and do business with people who make it easy to do business with them.

7. Expand our market sectors to break away from the competitors and enhance the focus on unattended areas.
8. Make learning a continuum so we will always be working on uncovering our weaknesses and our competitors', and identify gaps in our processes, our strategy, and our marketing.

Up to that point, all I really knew was how to build a sales organization in the consumer products, and food and beverage industries. Healthcare was a brand-new territory for me, but it was never intimidating.

It was both a great opportunity and a challenge to apply my own ideas and build a division of incredible significance. In the early days, I worked from sunup to sundown, seeking to understand how suppliers went to market and interacted with the diverse healthcare facilities.

Soon after my promotion, the company had me attend a large healthcare conference. Even though this was a conference and tradeshow we weren't directly involved in, I relished the opportunity and wanted to observe and soak up as much knowledge as possible, seeking out every opportunity to improve our effectiveness in the marketplace.

I remember coming back from the conference with stacks of supplier brochures and literature from different types of organizations. More importantly, the experience left me brimming with ideas. At first, the healthcare industry seemed highly complex and far-reaching, from the acute areas of single or multiple hospital systems to the non-acute areas of physician practices, surgery centers, assisted living centers, long-term care facilities, hospices, and so on. But soon, the industry structure became much clearer to me.

Sales of $82M meant we already had a good presence, but it was obvious we could do more. One weakness as an organization was that we weren't as focused as the number one and number two companies, and they had more people in sales. So, I worked my numbers, aiming to bring in 100 people dedicated to healthcare. This was about four times our competitors' combined numbers, and a key part of my burgeoning sales and marketing strategy.

Growing significantly inside a major corporate market called for dedicated sales resources. To accomplish this, I developed a 'train the trainer' format so more and more people would be focused on selling solely into the healthcare space. Armed with a detailed business plan requesting two or three dedicated people per distribution center, and with my boss's approval, I set up a meeting with our CEO where I would present my plan to him and discuss the details.

With only a week to prepare for the meeting, I spent the following days fine-tuning my ideas, laying out my exact objectives, and computing the numbers behind the resources needed to carry out this mission to elevate our place in the market. After all, I was asking for 100 highly skilled people to focus on a market with enormous potential.

The CEO was a straightforward, no-nonsense man who said he had no need for all the PowerPoint slides I had labored over in the early hours! I just had to tell him what I wanted and how my goals would be met.

He was highly intelligent, very business savvy, and quickly understood my plan. We sat in his office for over two hours discussing the business, my ideas, and our current market position. Clearly, he shared my enthusiasm for this new strategy.

Finally, he made his decision, which was to allocate one person per location, nowhere near my total of 100. My heart sank as I delicately challenged his decision, reiterating the required number of people to help elevate us to market leadership. I then told him these 100 people were really only the first phase! After that, we would add another 50-75 people based on expected sales growth.

Sticking my neck out far beyond my initial pitch, if he'd just provide me the resources to execute my plan, I promised him that the healthcare division would be his largest division in the company, and the market leader within five years. He looked at me long and hard and then smiled before he agreed. This was before he added, "Get me the sales, or your term here will be short!"

We shook on the deal, with his telling me to build a healthcare division that would be the envy of many for years to come. I left that meeting with more passion and drive to succeed than any time in my career thus far. The idea of being a 'short-timer' was a wonderful motivator, much better than being given a simple good luck message!

I formulated comprehensive job descriptions and job placement ads for each of our distribution centers, which they could post locally for experienced people proficient at selling into the healthcare market. Qualified candidates soon started surfacing and the regional General Managers were to conduct the first set of interviews. But I wanted to make the final decision on these key positions myself.

Failure through lack of talented and experienced staff wasn't going to be an option, so over the next 60 days, I conducted final internal interviews of over 200 people, with 80 or so making the final cut. A consistent go-to-market strategy was also in the works for all of these new reps, and soon it all fell into place. The buzz was so incredible that at times I was reluctant to leave the office, knowing that meeting my goals was closer than ever.

Key learning points for this chapter:

- Sometimes you have to go backwards for a short while to move forward later. Meet challenges as they come.
- If you move up to seeking sales from much bigger and challenging companies, make sure your approach and style are developed appropriately.
- Sometimes, there are different ways to look at your numbers to assess the value of the business you receive. Where margins are narrow, and volumes are high, Activity-Based Costing in relation to your processes can be a very useful and powerful tool.
- Never underestimate the need for planning. Any new challenges or existing ones need constant review and ongoing and appropriate goal-setting.
- When taking on new challenges, immerse yourself in building your knowledge as much and as quickly as you can—proactively seek to develop your own learning and don't wait around for others to teach you what you need to know.
- Check out your competition as thoroughly as you can. For those doing better than you, seek to understand as much as possible about how they achieved their success.

- To encourage growth, you must secure the appropriate resources to mobilize activity. It's an investment worth putting your best efforts into.

Case Study

Background

Via my consulting business, I worked with a company who manufactured and sold solar panels. They were making solid profits, and certainly had the drive, capacity, and infrastructure to do more.

The company was well set up, had a good product range, attractive brochures, and a good website, but something was missing. They still weren't leveraging all their potential opportunities to expand their business.

Approach

"Did you know that statistics show that a good deal of your income could come from the five people that you hang around with the most?" I asked their management team.

I was, of course, referring to their network, which they weren't using anywhere near as effectively as they could. They had to connect with key people in more powerful circles of influence, leading them later into networking with high-ranking government officials who were affiliated with critical decision makers. I wanted them to get into the education and healthcare markets.

Once they got their initial contacts, I encouraged them to nurture the relationships, so these people could understand better what their company could offer. When they gained visibility, they started getting government grants and funding, and with that they got access to making governmental bids.

They didn't win all of them, but it certainly got them on the right people's radar. Sometimes though, they'd be too cautious or underestimate their abilities to deliver, and that's where they needed a real push to grab great opportunities and take calculated risks.

"We are not sure we can handle this," one of the team said to me one day when a new bid had come in.

"Okay," I said. "We'll look at the opportunity and then we will dissect it to see what you can and can't handle?"

"Well, we're not quite there yet because we don't have enough people, we are not in that geography, we are not ..." and on he went with more "we are not" excuses.

"Well, what if we turn that 'we are not' into 'we will' and project into the future and respond?" I argued, remembering the bids I made in the past. "Work out what you need to put in place and how long you've got to do it. If you win the bid, you'll be ready by the time the work needs to start!"

Outcome

They went after the most coveted account and won. Since then, they've continued to chase every opportunity, increasing their profit by several million dollars. Sometimes, we have to push ourselves out of our comfort zones to grow. If we always stick to what's comfortable, then we aren't pushing ourselves hard enough.

2

SUCCESS DOES BREED SUCCESS

"If opportunity doesn't knock, build a door."

Milton Berle

ALTHOUGH WE WERE a Fortune 50 company with a very large marketing department, our prior marketing efforts for the healthcare division were almost non-existent. A meeting with the marketing heads granted me their support for a variety of initiatives, including the design of a marketing brochure, supporting promotional materials for my division, and a comprehensive marketing strategy.

Subsequently, we developed what we all thought was a good, comprehensive set of marketing collateral for our end-users to see how we were different from our competitors, and a strategy to market this newly formed division. The sales team liked the brochures, and so did our target clients. Even more so after we personalized our approach.

That change came from one of the most valuable lessons for me at that time, something I continue to teach others today: You must understand your customers and anticipate *their* needs.

We had our main brochure, and we thought it worked pretty well until a customer said to me, "You really don't understand our business, do you?" I was about to challenge him but stopped myself to let him continue. "We are a physicians' practice, and this brochure is for a *hospital*."

As soon as possible, I met with the Director of Marketing, and we agreed to develop another, more thorough marketing strategy that focused on customer type or sector and included acquisition and retention campaigns, along with new marketing collateral. We then created a number of different versions of the brochures according to the type of customer that was being targeted.

Whether it was a physicians' practice, surgery center, nursing home or hospital, the major sectors had their own customized brochure. The real differences between the materials were minor, but they varied as necessary for the different markets. Mostly, it was as simple as using different photos and headings, and specific healthcare jargon, but our customers now felt that we understood them better and thus, could satisfy their needs. Selling is about understanding and fulfilling a need; it was a simple technique that exploded our sales.

In addition to the tailored marketing material, we also started forming alliances with specialized medical groups such as MGMA (Medical Group Management Assn), FASA (Federated Ambulatory Surgery Assn), FAH (Federation of American Hospitals), HIGPA (Health Industry Group Purchasing Association), and many more. Our ads began to appear in various magazines and publications, and we were the first vendor in our category to do that. We also started participating in trade shows and conferences, and within two years, our competition followed suit. As is often said, being copied is one of the best forms of flattery.

As time passed, the volume of information and data we were gathering was so big it was becoming unwieldy. The creation of one sales tool and related marketing led to more facts and figures, so managing the database for leads and contacts was becoming a nightmare since they needed constant updating. A more efficient solution was needed.

After roughly six months of quietly working behind the scenes with my National Accounts Administration Manager, we unveiled a state-of-the-art, comprehensive intranet site for our reps to have every single sales resource only a click away. There was nothing like it, even in the design stage, on our competitors' radar. We had more than 100,000 records fully categorized and instantly available to our staff. With all the collateral and marketing now at our fingertips, we just had to go out and secure deals successfully.

As a critical knowledge management tool, our intranet served as a resource library and even published information about our advertisements could be accessed from this system. It was always a good selling point if you asked the customer if they'd seen a particular ad in a certain magazine and could present it at a moment's notice.

While our comprehensive data storage system kept various types of information readily available to our salespeople, we still needed more. The next development was a CRM (Customer Relationship Management) system that tracked sales force activity and progress with prospective customers. This interactive tool alerted us to customers whose buying activity had changed for a variety of reasons.

In our relentless pursuit of being the best in the marketplace, we were always looking for something different to stay several steps ahead of the competition. One of the highest potential areas we identified was the non-acute market of doctors' offices, clinics, and so on, where they were decentralized in their purchasing decisions.

After understanding how the Group Purchasing Organizations (GPO's[1]) worked, we realized that they did a poor job of educating their affiliates (outside the hospitals) about their contract portfolios. For instance, the non-acute practices could buy bandages and gauze via a contract already negotiated by the GPO, but because of poor communication they were unaware of that, so they would buy their bandages from anyone who walked in the door and seemed to offer a good price.

I decided to formulate an entire line of related medical products that were still inside our core competency, such as medical disposables. Now that we had an established product line, we could now offer the value proposition of vendor consolidation by streamlining their ordering process, while allowing us to obtain larger rebates through greater volume.

I added thousands of medical products from roughly twenty suppliers for our reps to sell. It is only in the last two years or so that this been adopted by other big players as a strategy. At the time, it was amazing that our biggest competitors were still focused

1 A GPO is an entity that helps healthcare providers-such as hospitals, nursing homes and home health agencies-realize savings and efficiencies by aggregating purchasing volume and using that leverage to negotiate discounts with manufacturers, distributors and other vendors.

on major hospitals in the acute market. Having the membership rosters of the GPO's on hand, the potential numbers were far larger on the non-acute side.

One of the lessons that came with the development of the medical products line was that the faster we reached the decision maker, the quicker they'd made a decision, resulting in a higher margin. Within 18 months, we captured the market and were selling over $100M annually in this category alone.

It helps to observe your competitors' behavior, and, as I'll discuss more in Chapter 7, we all like to fish where the big fish are, and in my case at that time, it was the hospitals. However, in many markets, for every big fish, there are also hundreds of little ones, and you can still get full on those. As well as making initial sales, this approach increases your market presence and awareness with the big fish, creating momentum in gaining their business as well.

I won't belabor every single thing we did, but rather skip forward three years to when we started winning major recognition awards from various GPOs. The first was 'Supplier of the Year,' which was granted to us by the largest GPO in the industry.

The following year we received two more awards from other GPO's, with the most rewarding being 'Med-Surg Supplier Of The Year'. This was especially significant since there were much bigger companies whose primary focus were products in these specific categories, yet we were competing right in their space.

This was a statement to the industry as a whole that we were now a serious player, and my boss and the CEO were more than satisfied with our results. With no thought of my being a 'short-timer' anymore, my passion for growth and excellence was almost becoming an obsession.

Our next initiative was to create the *Top Prospect Program*, which centered on the training of our sales organization throughout all our locations. We had them focus on marketing to around 800 hospitals, a systematic and relentless campaign of promotion after promotion every quarter.

This campaign's objective was to make sure our brand was always visible to these customers, so our name came up first whenever they needed to order anything. This increased our business significantly, and to mark this achievement, when our biggest customer reached the hundred-million-dollar mark in purchases, we had bottles of wine engraved with our logo and 'Thanks A Hundred Million.' After presenting the first bottle to that company's CEO, he teased that our name was everywhere as if it were written in graffiti on their walls. Our campaign was an overwhelming success, but it didn't stop there.

We had grabbed so much of the market that I decided that it was time to capitalize on our overall position in the healthcare industry. Our ads were already appearing in center-page spreads in the magazines of the largest healthcare goods supplier, but I still wanted to confirm our position as the premier healthcare supplier, with regards to the size of our presence, and the impact and experience our customers realized from doing business with us. It had to be something our competitors hadn't done yet.

The opportunity presented itself while we were planning for the next trade show. Usually, a company pays for one or two booths, so I had our marketing people book a space large enough for twenty booths. We set up our area right in the middle of the convention hall and created a new program inside of our healthcare division called *The Strategic Healthcare Partner Alliance Program*. The booths in our space were then offered to our alliance suppliers, with the guarantee that they would have no competing suppliers in the alliance program. Each of our participating suppliers paid for their own booth within our larger space.

Getting into this Alliance Program became a key goal for our suppliers since members had greater exposure, granting them more ways to sell their product, which in turn benefited our company. This made our presence infinitely more impressive than our competitors' little booths and clearly became *the* dominant force at all the GPO trade shows that year.

Another plus was that this approach didn't increase our marketing budget because our partners paid for their share of the space. It was all about leveraging the assets you already have to gain a wider presence.

Planning ahead and creatively using available resources is the key to staying on top of your game. Our competitors were continually trying to catch up to us, while we were already pushing our boundaries further and further out. Also, running the biggest division granted me access to the top of our company. Since I delivered on my promises, I could employ more people when the need arose, and other members of our team were prepared to stick their necks out for me. My allies increased, backing me up as they understood that it would benefit them in return.

This give-and-take dynamic is crucial, especially in a large company where everything is usually done according to set procedures and protocol. If you can deliver on your business plan, you will get the resources needed to deliver on your next initiative.

I would communicate that I could get things done by dedicating the time and resources, training the team, and giving them the appropriate sales tools, and implementing a comprehensive program in marketing, sales, and distribution. Tie all these together, and you have a core vision of purpose that you can sell like mad.

And we did. We also started a telesales division within the company, which also proved highly successful. But despite our flourishing success, it wasn't right to just sit back and watch the business take care of itself. Every milestone, every achievement had to be consolidated and used to develop newer strategies.

When you deliver huge results and help a company become more successful, you reap the rewards. Even though I initially took a pay cut and filled a lower position at our company, my instincts told me that this was a far more progressive company that would give me room to grow, and I did, both financially and experientially.

Our strategy was clearly working, but I felt it could still use another new marketing tactic. The one I decided on would be both expensive and risky; nevertheless, I arranged a healthcare conference in the Boston Harbor Hotel and invited the CEOs of 80 major health companies.

Designed to be a truly memorable event, I even felt that the hotel chairs weren't up to the right standards. So, we had them replaced with big, high-backed leather chairs from one of our Strategic Healthcare Alliance Partners. We invited speakers like the Surgeon General of the United States and the Chief Medical Officer of the AMA (American Medical Association), so we had the undivided attention of the most senior people in the hospitals' and doctors' community.

After the conference, there was a private dinner party for the top twenty CEOs. A separate invitation was sent to them with no specific information, except they were invited to an exclusive dinner that started promptly at 6:00 p.m. When everyone was seated and waiting, there was one empty seat at the table. The door opened, and in walked our special guest, Robin Williams. He went around the table, roasted the CEOs, and performed his trademark antics.

Dinner with Robin Williams and the rest of the event cost $100,000, but as a result, eleven of the twenty CEOs gave us a combined total of new business worth about $20 million. Now that was a *very* good return on our investment.

Of course, not all our ideas were that grand, and some of them were quite gimmicky, such as the fake cola can that played the *Mission Impossible* theme song. This was around the time of Tom Cruise's first *Mission Impossible* movie, and my business card stated that with our company every mission was possible.

Even though it was gimmicky, it opened doors for us. We spent a few thousand dollars on the campaign and gained a couple of million dollars in business. The best thing about the marketing campaigns, besides the business they brought in, was that they were a lot of fun. If you don't enjoy what you do every day, what's the point?

The success of our strategies depended on careful and thorough planning, each element being continually updated with our market and competition in mind. Every facet was covered: what the collateral marketing should look like, what medium we would use for advertising, how we presented ourselves at trade shows, what value proposition we should be articulating, and which markets we should be focusing on. Our aim was to capture the market and call it our own, which we achieved.

When I attended a conference and liked what someone else was doing, I would implement it in our company. But whatever idea that was, it was carefully restructured to meet our goals, so it would eventually be transformed into an original concept. This kept our company ahead of our competitors, and by the time they copied one of our ideas, we had already moved onto something newer and better.

As the division grew, so did our marketing budget. And the more money we spent, the more we expanded. It was always challenging, but it was still always fun. In the ten years that I was in the healthcare division of the company, our sales grew from $82 million to over $600 million. Within a two-year period, we came to lead the non-acute market, where the majority of the total expense in healthcare comes from.

But our success was not just from the products we were selling, but from forging enough new paths in healthcare to turn us into a market leader. My personal success in the company came from delivering on my promises and surrounding myself with very talented people with whom I had great working relationships. They all knew healthcare was *the* best sales division to be part of in the company.

Key learning points for this chapter:

- When developing your marketing materials, make sure they specifically address your primary clients. If you have different client groups, then don't make your materials too generic.

- Selling is about understanding and fulfilling known needs, so ensure your marketing materials clearly address those.
- Set yourself apart from your competitors in a positive light and leverage as many options as possible to generate company and brand awareness.
- The greater your success, the more data you will amass on customers, prior sales, communications, and so on. Ensure that you have the best possible customer relationship management system, so you can integrate this information into future accounts when needed.
- The market you are currently working in may be saturated with competitors. Always be on the lookout for new market opportunities, especially where the competition is less fierce, so you'll have more leeway to position yourself as a market leader.
- When you identify new and highly valuable opportunities, be relentless in your pursuit of business. Find new ways to motivate and reward your salespeople as they seek new avenues to raise brand and product awareness.
- Pushing the boundaries of your marketing strategy can be expensive and risky, but it can bring equally serious results. If it's appropriate and affordable, with a clearly defined potential return, don't be afraid of doing something big and radically different.
- You can never plan and re-plan enough for your marketing to keep on top of things—continually refresh your databases and pools of information, seeking every opportunity to stay ahead of your competition.
- No matter whom they are made to, success comes from delivering on promises and surrounding yourself with equally successful people.

Case Study

Background

One of my clients was involved in the leasing side of the real estate business, which had been considerably successful for fifteen years. However, while she knew that both she and her company could do more, she felt stuck.

Approach

"What do you love to do?" I asked her during one of our conversations.

"Well …I love to talk to people, to interact with them," she replied before adding with a laugh, "and I love to make money!"

"What we need to do is to attract more people who'll want to talk with you and connect with you. That means we need to build your brand. It's not just about marketing your company; it's about *you*."

First, I introduced her to a social media specialist who worked on her website and connected it to her Facebook page and social media. Then we got a spot on the local radio.

"On Saturday mornings people are very often in their cars, but surprisingly, that time is not nearly as expensive as during the working week. Let's see if we can get an interview with one of the top local talk shows and observe how it goes in raising your profile. Would you be okay doing that?"

"Well, sure," she replied, looking fairly relaxed at the idea.

"How about speaking? As in public speaking?"

"I guess I'd be okay, but I'd need some help," she answered, now a little more hesitantly.

"I have just the right people in mind," I told her.

The local branch of Toastmasters, a global organization with over 330,000 members specializing in public personality development, leadership, and communication skills was the perfect platform to help her improve her public speaking. Here, people can practice their speeches in a safe environment and receive feedback from their peers. This soon proved to be a great success for her.

After getting her on the radio, we developed her speaking skills so she could start delivering presentations and speaking at seminars and conferences. Her Facebook following was starting to build nicely, with her social media presence boosted by traditional advertising involving plenty of signs about her and her company around town.

All that speaking practice helped her come out of her shell and become more confident in one-on-one situations as well. I needed her to feel more comfortable with approaching and conversing with strangers because it was time to attack who we identified as her target market. This was the local affluent people, but especially women since studies showed that they tended to be more involved in real estate than their husbands.

She began to turn up at the best local country clubs and get involved with several women's groups there. Soon her newfound connections added to her expanding client base. Before this,

she used to lease houses to middle-income earners but quickly became a sought-after property manager for high-end homes supporting the upper echelons of the local society.

Outcome

Having built herself a platform from which to progress, through brand recognition enhancement and building professional skills, she now attracts high-end clients, not just locally but from all over the world. She's now known as the best in class in their market. In just a few years, she more than tripled her business and is now grossing more than $3M annually.

3

UPHILL BATTLES HAVE TO BE FOUGHT SOMETIMES

"Our greatest weakness lies in giving up. The most certain way to succeed is always to try just one more time."

Jim Ryun

THERE ARE A number of aspects to building a business. You need to develop a solid business plan and a unique strategy. You must have all the right processes in place and employ the right people, with the proper measurements that can be used to motivate staff and generate the right behavior. Of course, it's also essential to have a product that creates a difference in the marketplace.

Early in my career, I had recognized that you had to have all of the above as foundational. While still learning the ropes, sometimes my processes were faulty while the people and products were good. Or the processes and products were good, but the people needed better alignment to the company strategy and overall vision. All of these are mission-critical aspects of a business that must be fully addressed, and my next job confirmed that if all of the above were out of sync with each other, an organization would inevitably struggle.

The healthcare division I built and managed became successful because we had a strategy, a solid and executable business plan, and good people who were rewarded and compensated well based on their efforts and successes. All the processes were in place and working harmoniously with each other. Then the company decided to purchase a larger brand on a huge scale, and that was the trigger for my moving on.

The organization's goal was to leapfrog the competition as an entire company and not just the healthcare division. So they purchased an organization that was, in effect, their least expensive competitor. They could have easily afforded to buy better, considering their recent massive growth in all their markets, but unfortunately, the organization and brand they purchased was not only the least expensive, but also the least respected. As a result of the acquisition, the company was never the same again and started selling products of lesser repute.

The acquisition decision had further implications with the resignation of our CEO and the drastic change in the company dynamics. The employees of the newly purchased company had a vastly different perspective and approach to business from ours. Their mindset, lack of understanding as to quality and culture, transformed our former interactions and processes into an entirely new company. It was all very alien to me, making it the right time for me to seek new ground.

After a few months, I was hired by the president of another equipment supply firm to help build and run their healthcare division. Even though they had some issues from an organizational and operational standpoint, they had a great reputation for superior products, and I was excited to have new challenges.

Theirs was a very competitive market, so they kept abreast of their competitors' activities as their forward-thinking designers worked constantly to develop new innovations. Thus, they had first-class products, but there were some complications regarding their people and processes. This quickly became evident to me after I began working there.

First, there was my boss. When I began to put forward ideas to be implemented in the healthcare division, he questioned me on what I thought his role was within the organization. Since no one had informed me of his position and title, I came to learn in an awkward and uncomfortable situation that he ran the healthcare division.

Instead of leading the healthcare division, my position turned out to be second-in-command, and my new boss knew virtually nothing about healthcare. Someone hadn't exactly been truthful about my role, or at the very least they had some serious internal communications problems. After working under my boss for only a few months, I had enough.

The president, who had interviewed me, listened to my emphatic—and clearly reasonable—objections about reporting to someone who didn't know his business. Within a week, they reassigned him to another project, and I secured the role of the National Director of Healthcare.

While the president of the company was a pleasant, well-intentioned, and hard-working person, he was also a micromanager. Unfortunately, this manifested itself throughout the company.

Micromanagement stifles all creativity and can be a major source of growth-related problems because management feels the need to control every aspect of what the staff does, down to the smallest detail. As a result, it slows down processes, efficiency, and ultimately, overall productivity.

Despite having a certain amount of autonomy in my position, I still felt somewhat smothered, especially after enjoying the freedom that came with my former roles. I tried educating people on different aspects of healthcare, group hosting organizations, and the need for contracts, but ultimately though, it would be a struggle to replicate my previous successes in such a command-and-control environment. Not surprisingly, the company had a high staff turnover.

As mentioned, they did make good products, and some were exceptional; it was the process and management issues that held them back from attaining their full potential in the market. As an example, the company would sometimes ship out products knowing there were missing parts! If it weren't for their products' excellent functionality and performance, and tenacious staff who were committed to the organization, they'd have struggled to keep their heads above water.

To grow in this field, our division had to act as a separate entity and do things differently from the rest of the established system. Eventually, I brought in a talented product designer who had the right healthcare technical background and a great work ethic. He started redesigning and improving one of our potential market-leading products until we realized we were wasting our time.

I learned that our company was working on the same product with another company whose technology was more leading edge. To compound this, they also became a competitor since the person on our company's end who negotiated the agreement didn't make the contract watertight. Soon the company who was producing our product managed to produce and sell a better one themselves, and there was no way we could play catch up.

People, process, product. The sales contract was flawed, the process needed to be streamlined, and we needed a new and better product in the market ASAP. After developing a plan to expand in other areas of healthcare, we began working on a different product which we were sure could be used to gain market awareness and market share. It was time to make this one a real success and take some of the other good products with it.

The company had about twenty offices around the country and more in Europe. All these markets became my basis for a strategic business model that would let us hire new people or move key employees into healthcare specialist positions.

First, I focused on high-density markets and creating appropriate job descriptions, so our in-house recruitment company could seek out potential candidates. The recruitment division actively helped weed out unqualified candidates, leaving me to conduct final interviews for a particular market. It took a little longer than expected due to some of our internal processes, but within five months we had a small but strong sales management team in place, with 75% of the markets covered with experienced salespeople.

We developed marketing materials specific to each product and sector, plus a comprehensive healthcare portal on the company website so end users could see and understand the technology by virtually displaying its various forms and functions.

The National Training Director also collaborated with our team in developing internal and external training guides and sales tools. From my previous working relationships, I got two GPO's to take on more of our products. So within my two years of working for this company, sales went from almost zero to nearly $50M annually. However, attaining this was mostly an uphill battle.

From a job satisfaction perspective, this was the most challenging point of my career. The organization was a good subject for examining issues in running a company, especially in their relationship with the workforce. Micromanagement was rampant on every level, and decision-makers still needed essential and fundamental knowledge in marketing, sales, and other aspects of the entire process. All these resulted in high staff turnover. Considering my previous ten years and earlier roles, this greatly tested my self-motivation, pushing me harder than ever to focus on the customer, what I wanted to provide them with, and the end results.

One day, while in route to a healthcare conference in Barcelona, I received a call from a past colleague. He wanted to discuss the finer points of starting a national accounts division for the non-profit cooperative he moved into, and we agreed to meet the next time I was in Chicago. This timely opportunity to develop an effective and meaningful enterprise was a massive boost to my morale.

Two weeks later, we discussed the project's details over dinner. It was a corporation that acted as a non-profit and comprised a large number of independent stationers, and office furniture and equipment suppliers. They had 'shareholders' in the form of hundreds of members who each owned their own company, distributing office products, paper, technology, and other related goods. He needed my help in creating an organization with a national accounts program like in the company where we previously worked together.

The independent dealers traditionally focused on their own city or town, and this corporation offered them the chance to have a much larger footprint. He wanted me to develop the systems, processes, and marketing, basically everything needed to secure national contracts. After discussing it for about six weeks, this was now my chance to build something great again—minus unnecessary barriers and constraints—and I gladly handed in my notice.

The first few days were spent in absorbing and observing this new company's system. In fact, my very first day was spent at the corporation's board meeting with many of the key shareholders, allowing me to get a better understanding of what the organization was all about. The following week, I visited their Indianapolis headquarters and became immersed in building this new national sales division.

I barely started in the role when a major business opportunity came my way and, despite our unprepared state, I could not let it slip by. The potential client was the largest U.S. buying cooperative with about twenty suppliers inside their portfolio, some of whom had contracts up for renewal, and they were looking for new bids. This was my chance to make a pitch for their office products, computer technology, and furniture.

Our bid response would be several hundred pages long, and so one of the first people I hired to assist me, because she was knowledgeable in the entire procedure, was my administrator from the original healthcare company. She raised an eyebrow after learning that we would have to answer questions as if everything in our plan already existed. But she was also sure that we'd deliver, so she came on board.

Working on the bid was a mad dash! I was calling on potential team members left and right, composing job descriptions, and preparing for other future recruits while our bid response was in the works. When it looked like we were about to complete the bid—with all its talk of the teams we had in place—is when I started sending out job offers!

Our bid response came in at around 300 pages, setting out our overall capabilities, value proposition, and of course, pricing. Having a large national piece of business was not uncommon for my new employer, as they had held federal government contracts for nearly a decade, but nothing on this scale.

The large cooperative got back in touch within only three weeks of our submission, with questions about our bid. That definitely boosted team morale, and we held a number of discussions over the next two weeks. Then I got another call to set up a meeting with the cooperative and other key members of our board; this would be the final, make-or-break session.

I was in Chicago, and the President and Executive VP were on the line from Indianapolis. While waiting for the call, the upcoming project's magnitude finally hit me hard, and I realized that this was the biggest business day of my life—our bid was more than $519M … annually!

Our conference call started, and various questions were being thrown back and forth. The moment of truth arrived when I asked, "Who else are you considering for this award?"

Their answer floored me. "No one, just you, if you make it out of these final discussions." I went fishing and just caught the biggest whale in the ocean!

We won the bid and soon began building the team, one much bigger than a sales organization. It took several days of rigorous training, setting up a distribution network, and wording on a very sophisticated e-Commerce platform to support our distribution partners. We were actually building a whole company within a few short weeks! But we lived up to our promise in the bid, and soon after that, contract after contract after contract headed our way.

Because of our new national infrastructure, we created specialized policies and procedures. Ours was a national e-Commerce platform that granted our customers a shared and unified experience. What was unique about this was that we utilized technology to allow for centralization, enabling us to have full control over the entire system, despite hundreds of servicing partners on the backend. Our products were still delivered by local independent business parties (servicing partners) and the profits generated from their sales were kept in the local economy.

It was a win-win situation for everyone after my team pulled off that huge bid. We had rolled up our sleeves and got down to work until the entire project was in place. However, the aftermath was almost anticlimactic and once again, the question arose: "What's next?"

This time, it was my wife, Deborah, who answered it. Understanding my urgency to always do something new and different, she made some radical suggestions as we were driving to a dinner party one evening.

"You have made billions of dollars for the companies you've worked at over the span of your career, yet your salaries and bonuses have not been aligned with the massive revenue contributions that you've made," she said, looking at me from the passenger seat. "You should set up your own business and become a consultant for other companies and make them all wildly successful as you've done over and over again in your previous positions."

What she said struck a chord with me, but I wasn't convinced immediately and mumbled, "Maybe …"

"Oh, come on Kevin," she chided. "It will be immensely more fulfilling, and you'll be compensated much more richly than if you worked for someone else. You're exceptionally dedicated and committed, hard-working, passionate, and enormously talented and good at what you do. You're ready for so much more."

It took a little bit of time, but Deborah eventually convinced me that perhaps it was time to take another leap of faith like I did with that pay cut many years ago.

Key learning points for this chapter:

- ❖ In any successful business, there will be the right people, the right product, and the right processes—always try to ensure that you have the best mix of all these critical components.
- ❖ When operating in a highly competitive market, always seek to understand where your competitors are strongest, so you know where your own best opportunities may lie.

- ❖ Micromanagement stifles creativity. Ensure that you are not too hands-on and give your people breathing space so that their natural creativity can work in your best interest.
- ❖ The best in products need the best in designers. Hire product designers and developers who fully understand what you want and what your market needs. If you enter into partnerships for this, make sure your contracts are watertight.
- ❖ When building new teams, always give them the best support regarding training, tools, and processes.
- ❖ When major opportunities arise, no matter how unprepared you feel, grasp them with both hands. Always remember that more often than not, without risk there cannot be reward.
- ❖ If you find new opportunities and know what needs to be done, don't be afraid to take all necessary steps to secure them, despite apparent setbacks and difficulties.

Case Study

Background

One of my clients, who still works with me from time to time, has a great family company based on the U.S. East Coast. They run a manufacturing business and also import goods from China and Taiwan.

When I was first asked to work with them, they had roughly twelve employees and about $7M in sales. The company founder had passed the business to his son, who was the President and CEO at the time. They had good depth of product and a relatively strong brand, but a solid growth strategy was much

needed. They wanted to try to double if not triple the size of the company; this is where I came in.

Approach

When I first evaluated the situation, it almost seemed that they had been reasonably successful despite themselves. They didn't have any systematic processes in place to get things done efficiently and consistently, and they had numerous personnel problems, especially with a sales manager who didn't act like one. They also had independent sales reps that managed their particular territory in whatever way they saw fit.

As discussed in this chapter, building an effective organization depends on product, people, and processes. They already had a good product, so we needed to work on the remaining two. After discovering all these issues, I spoke to the CEO.

"This place is simply disorganized. We need to put together a solid business plan for at least the next five years. To back that up we need to put together a proper organizational structure, with clear responsibilities and accountabilities—and all that needs to be communicated to everyone."

"But we have ..." he began, but my smile and upturned palm signaled for him to let me continue. He nodded.

"We need to get our arms around policies and procedures so that we can make this company run like a single, cohesive unit that truly knows where it's going and how it's going to get there. We need everything from structure charts to job descriptions to performance matrices ..."

A pause.

"And your sales manager needs to start acting like a sales manager."

Understandably, that was tough, but he needed to hear that. If he wanted to upgrade the business worth to $20M, then his current sales manager was not the guy to do it.

"But he's been ..." he began again but stopped himself this time.

"You started your financial year several months ago. I asked for his budgets and projections, and I'm still yet to see them if they exist at all. How can you run a business like that?"

I asked him how he managed the sales reps, and he said he couldn't hold independent contractors accountable for their actions. My answer to that was "Of course you can! Do you know that only three of the nine sales reps are delivering? This company desperately needs to put a sales plan together."

While the sales manager was very talented from an industry knowledge perspective, he was not cut out for the role he was in. Pushing him didn't work, so the CEO had to let him go, even though he was considered a highly valued employee. It just had to be done.

Once we got over that obstacle, I helped the CEO recruit someone who fit the role better and could take the business to a higher level in sales. We started drawing up proper budgets and projections, provided sales reps with better tools for selling their products and services, and also came up with a revised compensation package so that they could be better motivated.

Their new manager went out on the road with them to help build a sense of teamwork through joint efforts.

Outcome

We ended up replacing much of the initial staff—it was necessary, and the CEO came to recognize that. And while they haven't quite tripled their business yet, they've certainly doubled it. In 2015, they won an independent award for being the best company in their industry and are still on a great trajectory for substantial growth in the coming years.

This CEO had significant uphill battles to face, but he did have some very good and competent people on his staff. We focused on using their strengths as a key point for turning the company around. Sometimes, you just have to strip an establishment to its foundation to be able to start to run a business effectively. When you cut your losses, in effect you are creating space for bigger gains to come.

4

Create Demand Through Innovation

"Innovation distinguishes between a leader and a follower."

Steve Jobs

IF WE TAKE a step back, my first job after college was a Regional Manager position in a beer brewing company, with the objective of starting the southwest sales region. Comprising four State areas, no previous market development had existed in this part of the country.

Now, it may sound like a pretty grand job title, but it was an entry-level sales position. I had become acquainted with the company at a career event in college, and when I joined them my main responsibilities involved sales. I was given that title because it suggested to potential customers that my position granted me the authority to assure them that our products were worth their investment.

This early experience taught me that if you give your employees a respectable-sounding title, they have a greater chance of capturing decision makers as their audience. Responsibilities notwithstanding, if I'd been given the title of Sales Representative instead of Regional Manager, our clients would have responded to me much differently. As they say, "perception is reality."

The way it works in the brewing business is that resellers (i.e., bars, gas stations, grocery stores, etc.) can only purchase their beer stocks from a distributor, in other words, they cannot buy directly from the manufacturer. Because of this, I had to work in cooperation with the resellers *and* distributors.

There were three major distributors in my region that provided beer for bars and grocery store chains that I had to convince to stock our product. My company had made some initial sales calls to these distributors, but they weren't getting traction for our beer because we hadn't established a reseller network. This whole situation gave me some very early lessons in supply chain management. In this scenario, we had to have the resellers lined up before distributors would be on board to stock our beer.

While I was young and still learning the ropes, my job required me to penetrate a tough market that was already dominated by the country's leading beers. Back then, I was less risk-averse than I am today, so the idea that I didn't have much to lose gave me the boldness needed to go out and secure our target market. I decided to try a different approach to selling our products.

My job was to create demand, with the understanding that the distributors only wanted to work with what they referred to as 'good customers,' that is, those who paid on time. A bar seeking to order from a distributor for the first time had to go through a credit approval process. This meant that I could potentially spend time pursuing relationships with bars that, in the end, would not be approved by the distributor.

The beer business is highly competitive. Much like today, in the early 1980s, resellers and distributors often operated with exclusive relationships with a manufacturer. For example, a bar would not sell two "competing" beer brands; just like certain hotels and professional stadiums today align themselves with one soft drink brand. Being new to the business, rejections came my way from left, right, and center, but this did not hinder my determination in the least. I had to adapt my approach rather than rattle out the same spiel to my prospects and expect the same results.

I was seeking to develop a pool of end-user resellers based on their relationships with specific distributors and began with attending trade shows and networking to facilitate brand awareness. I also made several cold calls to the top three distributors and convinced one of them to let me host a beer tasting at a popular bar. If it went reasonably well, they would provide me with limited distribution in Dallas until end-user demand warranted expansion … or elimination.

I befriended the owner of one of the trendiest bars in Dallas and offered him a couple of free kegs of beer for the tasting, but it was my other ideas that really sold him on the deal. While not quite Robin Williams, this was where my more radical ideas first came into play.

Some of the liquor companies that previously hosted tastings hired girls to walk around with little shot glasses to offer guests at the tasting venue, and this gave me an idea to take it a step further. Since this beer promotion was held in Dallas, I decided to hire several attractive bikini-clad models to emulate the Dallas Cowboys cheerleaders for the event. The tasting was a roaring success, the bar owner got his free kegs of beer, and we sold more beer at a small mark-up, above the distribution cost.

The next night I visited a different establishment that I frequented with friends. They had already heard about the successful event at the bar down the street, so they were eager to hold their own tasting.

One more factor that added to the success of these first two tastings was that I worked a deal with the models once they got on board with our team. The bar would pay them a nickel for every glass or bottle that was sold, which motivated the girls to work tirelessly in promoting our beer. The bar owners were very happy to oblige, and the models walked away with an extra hundred dollars between them.

I had tried convincing my company to give me a budget for the initial model hire, but they refused. So again, I had to be creative. Every month I was allocated two cases of beer for samples, plus two cases for my own personal consumption. To get the funds I needed, I sold my two personal cases and hired the first models from the proceeds, striking a deal with the girls that they would make a lot more money with my nickel incentive plan than the $20 I had paid each of them.

To accelerate demand, my mission for the week was to get as many bars around the city to hold tastings with as many models as I could hire. I spent my mornings making phone calls to potential bars and then visiting with them in the afternoon, explaining my approach to the owners. That first distributor had given me 90 days to build the right level of demand for him to carry our line. I hit the target within 60 days, but the pace of my efforts continued nonetheless.

I took my successes on the road to another distributor in Houston. I made my pitch with a simple report detailing the bar sales and told them about my promotional strategy with the tastings in Dallas. They gave me a list of contacts for about twenty bars and clubs, and my network slowly began to grow.

The next day I started calling these bar owners and managers, telling them I was referred by the distributor. On my first four phone calls they hung up on me, and the fifth started yelling. Needless to say, it was disheartening.

At first, I thought I wasn't doing anything different from my sales tactics in Dallas, and then it hit me: *I had not formed any initial relationships to open the doors.* It took me about three calls to club and bar owners back home to find a Houston connection. One available prospect was a warm lead, a friend's buddy, and after I called the guy and explained the situation, he asked me to stop by in a couple of days.

With two vacant days before my meeting, I returned to my hotel and using the telephone book listed the names and phone numbers of every bar, nightclub, and even strip joint in town. I figured that after I met with my friend's buddy, and also going on the assumption that we would set up a weekend event, I could conduct face-to-face cold calls until the end of the week. I was hopeful to be armed with a planned event at that first bar so the prospects I was calling on would see that their competitors had bought into the idea.

The afternoon of my meeting arrived, and I walked in decked out in my suit and tie. Nick, my friend's buddy I was meeting, acted a bit surprised. He pointed out that if I wanted to sell beer in his town, I should look like a local by putting on a pair of jeans. That sounded cool to me, but I knew that if my company supervisor ever found out, he would not like it.

My contact in Dallas, who connected me with Nick, had told him that our beer was selling well, and Nick liked my proven 'Dallas Business Plan'. Being a trendy bar, he said he could get the models and would be happy to pay them for what they sold.

My next task was to return to the Houston distributor and inform them of my success with Nick. But my eager anticipation of their being pleased was knocked back when I found out that Nick often didn't pay his distributor's bills on time, so they were less than excited to do business with him.

I called my boss about the situation, and he said we would talk to the distributor into giving Nick—based on my word—extended payment terms. I didn't tell the distributor that my boss had also mentioned that if Nick didn't pay up, it would be coming out of my pay check over the next 30 days. I was a little concerned, but I really did not have a choice, and my instincts were telling me things would be okay.

It took my company a while to set up the vendor paperwork with the new distributor but eventually, the Saturday of the first Houston tasting arrived. As I drove down from Dallas, I kept thinking about Nick's credit habits and that I might get stuck with paying for all that he sold. Once I arrived there, I stopped worrying as I got immersed in all the preparations.

When I had a chance to talk to Nick, I asked him about his beer order, and he showed it to me. My heart seemed to race and drop at the same time since I had never seen so much beer outside the plant at any one customer location. It seemed that he ordered a ton of beer, a dozen kegs, and cases upon cases of bottles. I was grinning from ear to ear and yet scared to death. If I had to pay for all of that, it would probably cost me four months' salary!

As soon as the event began, the bar started to fill up, and the models showed up in very skimpy bikinis; it was like an old college party on steroids. Within two hours of opening, the place was full, and I was pumped, but as fun as it was, I couldn't participate so I sat back and drank one iced tea after another. I finally left about 8:00 p.m., and the bar was still packed. I told Nick I would call him in the morning once I returned to Dallas.

On Sunday I called Nick several times but didn't get an answer. The same happened on Monday, and I began to panic thinking he'd shut down and that it was going to cost me a small fortune. On Tuesday I finally reached him and learned that he was off on Sundays, and the bar was closed on Mondays. I breathed a big sigh of relief. I asked him how the event went, and he said it was unbelievable; that he'd never sold so much alcohol at one time. Out of the dozen or more kegs he'd bought, all but two had gone, and all the cases had gone. He had about ten bottles in his cooler, and that was it.

A major triumph turned into an overwhelming success when he paid his bill to the distributor right on time. I had the largest single merchant order for the entire company U.S. wide that week.

A few weeks later, I'd signed up more bars in Houston, and when my boss came down to Dallas, I took him to all the bars that were now regularly serving our beer. He was singing my praises and then told me he wanted to go to Houston. That remark reminded me about my suit.

I told him I had to break company policy a bit. He suddenly had this serious look on his face, asking me what I'd done. So, I told him about wearing jeans, instead of my suit, after my first bar visit. After a brief pause, he laughed and said he thought I'd done something really stupid!

I had returned there before he arrived and picked up about ten more bars and clubs and then sealed three more deals the day we were together in Houston. There was no need for bikinis now, just traditional tastings plus word of mouth that people liked our beer was enough to sell our product.

Sales aggression coupled with the necessary networking had brought success, especially when—despite occasional rejection—they were aided by sheer persistence and determination. I started off by learning from our competitors that the way to market share is to create public demand and that I had to think on my feet. I needed to recognize that creativity to market a product or service was key. I also had to quickly grow volume coming from each distributor since I was paid on sales through them. My strategy was simply that more bars and tastings meant higher throughput and bigger sales.

Some years after all of this took place, I read a book which suggested that a major skill in business is to see an idea being used elsewhere and adopting and adapting that idea for your own company. That's just what I did with the models and bikinis; I took what was happening with liquor tastings, mixed in the cheerleaders, and there was my opportunity. Within a short space of time, I secured the three largest beer distributors in the region, which brought in tremendous sales once I demonstrated my commitment to them.

In writing this book, I want to show that success is what any person can achieve when they approach things the right way. All I have done, later in my career, and specifically at the outset with the beer company, is not rocket science. I also know I've been fortunate. But you need to apply some creative thinking. In college, I first considered law but decided it was too technical with no creativity, whereas business is about finding and implementing new ideas. It's more enjoyable if you do it right, but you also need tremendous perseverance.

Within a span of 18 months, I moved a brand-new multi-state area to become the second highest producing sales region in the U.S. That, of course, brought me to the attention of the executives at the company, and I got a call from one of their affiliate company presidents who needed help with a struggling division in the same part of the country.

Key learning points for this chapter:

- If you have employees in sales roles within your company, consider giving them job titles that will command respect from senior clients and be more likely to open doors to new opportunities.
- If you have suppliers that are essential to the success of your business, make sure you are equally devoted to keeping them happy as you are your clients. If your suppliers let you down, then your clients suffer.
- When you first start out in business, you need to be cautious, but that's also the time when you are going to need to be the least risk-averse. Believe in yourself and be confident.
- Driving up sales means creating demand, and more often than not, that needs creativity. Always look for different ways and opportunities to build success. Don't just look at what your competitors are doing, look at what the most successful companies are doing in different industries since ideas can always be adapted before being adopted.

- Building company and brand awareness is essential for new businesses. While cold calling cannot be avoided sometimes, greater opportunities to increase sales can come from leveraging the people that you know—*never* underestimate the power of networking.
- If you employ sales staff, even on a temporary basis, always look for ways to maximize their contribution through effective and innovative reward mechanisms.
- If you reach your target date earlier, don't stop and sit back congratulating yourself—increase the target and keep on working just as hard.
- This may sound simple and obvious, but when attending a meeting, dress appropriately for your client —a smart suit isn't always going to be best!

Case Study

Background

I had a client who was struggling in his car business, he worked very hard and did the best he could, but he couldn't get his business to grow.

He didn't have a car dealership in the traditional sense; he was more like a car broker working via the Internet. He had a supply of three to ten cars at any one time due to very limited cash flow and had to sell cars before he could go out and buy more.

Approach

When I first started working with him, I asked what he really wanted to be doing.

"Well, I would like to ultimately own my own dealership, away from operating solely via the Internet because it's hard for people to find me. I want my own place where in addition to selling cars I provide servicing, oil changes, tune-ups, and repairs. I want to start selling warranties on cars, too."

"Okay," I said, "but you're in a highly competitive market. I'll ask you what I always ask people, and that is, 'Who is your ideal customer?'"

I could tell he hadn't considered that angle, perhaps thinking that he could sell to anyone. He thought for a few moments and then nodded. When he spoke, he was again very decisive.

"My ideal customer is someone who's between 19 and 30 years old. It's someone who is just starting out with car ownership, doesn't have a ton of money, but wants to buy a pre-owned car in really good condition."

"Okay, so that's your target market, but how are you going to deal with these people? You know what people always say about used car salesmen right? How are you going to set yourself apart from your competition?"

Again, he pondered the question carefully before telling me that he didn't want to bombard people when they walked onto his lot. I asked him how he was going to do that when car salespeople are normally paid on commission. He answered more quickly this time.

"Of course it matters that people buy something, but my people are going to work on salaries. They are going to want to sell

a service as well as a car. I will have some sort of quota for car sales, but it is going to be more about the customer satisfaction."

This all sounded great, but to get it going, he needed a big improvement in his cash position so he could have a lot more cars to offer. I then asked him about where the biggest margins would be, and he told me it would be from more expensive cars.

Realization dawned: he might have to move up his target market age a little.

The math was simple. If he got $10,000 profit on a higher-end car, instead of having three or four cars, he could own five or six. That meant momentum because the more cars he could turn, the higher the profit, and the more cars he could buy.

"You know," I told him, "when you walk into a supermarket, you don't see three types of cereal for sale, you see twenty to thirty different options because variety sells. When you go into a successful car lot, you see dozens and dozens of cars, covering the niche manufacturers as well as the mainstream ones."

"But even with bigger margins, it's still going to take me a long time to get there and renting the space for a big lot is going to be way too much," he said, looking despondent again.

"For sure," I replied, "so we have to find a way to build the volume more quickly."

I got him to start networking with some of his competitors, suggesting that they put some of their cars on his lot for a percentage of the sale. He would not be making big margins off of their cars, but all of a sudden it would give him scale: instead

of having six cars he could have fifty and didn't need to put up the capital. It was a win-win situation for him and the other dealers, and when customers walked into his lot, it would look like all the cars were his.

He was surprised by how much his competitors took to the idea, something they'd never thought of before, so that meant he now needed to find a place to display all of these cars. Again, he saw this as a problem because even with a lot of cars for sale he would only be making the big margins on a few of them. My solution was to search for some underutilized space.

We found a showroom in a shopping mall that wasn't very old. The owner was having trouble renting out the space, but it had great visibility and curb appeal. What I suggested that he do was to propose to the owner that he pay him half the asking price for the first six months, and then every six months after that the rent could go up to a point where he might even be paying him more rent than what was currently being asked.

"That works for you on the front end and for him on the backend," I explained, "so it's a win-win, and it gives you time to build your business."

The mall owner agreed.

Outcome

Soon he had a great place for selling, with room for all the cars and the service bays as well. For him, the key was to leverage other people's assets towards building his own capital and brand. He created a niche because he knew who his target audience was,

and word went around that he was a more reasonable kind of used car dealer, not your typical hard-sell guy.

He got on social media to connect with the younger aspiring professionals that were his target market, to find and create more leverage opportunities. He started sponsoring events, and we set up a referral program to build brand loyalty: people would buy their first car from him and would change it every two to three years, so they remembered him as a reliable used car dealer.

Then we created more revenue streams when he made deals with the local car wash and with other car mechanics when his own service bays were fully booked. In not too long a time, he turned his two or three car sales a month into a multimillion-dollar business.

5

MAKE DREAMS A REALITY

"You must form a clear and definite mental picture of what you want; you cannot transmit an idea unless you have it yourself."

Wallace Wattles

THE NEXT STEP on my career ladder provided me with an opportunity to move into the food industry and join a different division of the beer company that was based in Birmingham, Alabama. This was a pizza-and-pasta business that had started as a franchise restaurant operation but moved into the custom food business where they sold all the ingredients for their products. Again, my title was Regional Manager to suggest that I was in a more senior role, but the new field of food represented some different challenges.

The people responsible for selling the product were independent distributors who had been assigned a geographical territory, targeting small stores or businesses like bowling alleys, skating rinks, and movie theaters that offered simple catering. The sales representatives each had a small warehouse or storage unit with walk-in freezers for the packages of ingredients, which they would take out on the road and sell.

While the company provided the trucks, their salespeople had to 'buy' the product before selling them and were only paid on a commission basis. What these independent distributors needed was to be more aggressive with their sales calls to potential customers in the area since they already had decent profit margins.

I was responsible for growing several different sectors based in nine geographic areas. Expansion meant adding more customers, and that needed more good people, which were difficult to find when there was no salary to offer. To make this work, I had to build a great team, but that certainly wasn't easy with that type of compensation plan. I had to show them that I was working for them and helping them grow their business.

To achieve exponential growth, I worked out that the company had to move away from the small stores and recreation hubs and get into the bigger grocery stores and supermarkets. I had to have volume and a lot more customers, and I wasn't going to achieve that with establishments that sold only a few units per week. Then there was the fact that the distributors spent too much time driving around for small orders.

Working my supply chain, I started to get involved with food brokers to get some traction by selling into the bakery and deli areas inside the supermarkets. We wanted them to stop selling frozen pizzas and make fresh ones using our ingredients but selling them under their own label.

The food broker approach was about getting a foot in the door. They already represented several companies whose products they sold to the supermarkets, which meant that they already had partnerships with places we were trying to move into. Some food brokers can be very large and some quite small, but all we needed was to get them to focus more time on selling our products and gaining new distribution outlets. Once that was accomplished, it would be up to my people to keep the orders coming.

Soon, we were working with a number of the food brokers and their staff. We'd host big launch days in supermarkets where we would hold pizza-making demos with our ingredients. Using our own little pizza ovens, we were soon moving hundreds of pizzas, even thousands, over some weekends.

It was during one of these events that I got to know an older gentleman with years of experience as a food broker who taught me a lot, especially about people skills. He was very well respected and a kind, soft-spoken guy. Through his friendly and jovial personality, I learned that you don't have to keep pounding people to make the sale.

According to him, I was going to have to make people "love me to death" and then they would buy from me. He said that I'd always get a lot of 'no's' in my life, but that I was going to get 'yeses' too, and that for every "no" I was one step closer to a "yes." As Napoleon Hill once said, "The better portion of all sales is made after people had said 'no.'"

During my stint at the beer company, I had to do quite a bit of grassroots selling, but I wasn't serving beer and dealing directly with people coming into the bars. With the pizza company, I learned that sometimes you need to roll up your sleeves and help with the grunt work. I must have rolled out thousands of pizzas, which taught me not to be afraid to get my hands dirty or think any task was beneath me. In a nutshell, it was about leading by example. It gained me the respect of my own people *and* the food brokers when I showed them that I wasn't afraid of hard work.

Another thing I learned from that gentleman was something I still do today with many of my consulting clients, and that is seeing the broader view. I am fortunate to be what I call a big-picture and futuristic thinker, and I applied this skill in a difficult recruitment process.

What I did was discuss a scenario to get potential recruits to realize that they could make as much money as they wanted if they were willing to put their best efforts in. I wanted them to envision themselves with that new car or bigger home and understand that they were actually in a better position to get that than someone with a salary.

If they were going to wait for the sales to come in, they'd go nowhere fast, so they always had to look for opportunities and new ideas to make the situation work for them. I had a small salary myself and told them how I had solved a problem I knew they must also be facing.

My salespeople were provided a truck, but they had to pay for their own gas. I was in the same place. The company reimbursed our gas money but wouldn't give us a credit card. I was burning through gas, literally and figuratively, like crazy, and it was difficult to allot an extra budget for that.

Near my apartment complex was a gas station that I frequented, so I befriended the owner and eventually earned his trust. I reached the point where I was confident enough to ask if I could start an account with him. He said yes, which solved my cash flow problem by allowing me to utilize someone else's money to work for me.

I'd use this example to demonstrate to my recruits and teammates how I identified an opportunity, developed it, and made it work for me. If present circumstances aren't going the way you want them to, look for an opportunity that can result in the outcome that you want. Any business needs to manage its cash flow, which is what I was doing by finding alternative ways to generate disposable funds. Today, I still teach my clients about the need to find ways to leverage other people's money.

I interviewed several people, having them visualize my value proposition by articulating what we were about. I was selling myself, but as I look back, I was also selling a dream that had to come alive. In the same way as my writing this book, it was all about the words I used to get people to believe in the vision and themselves.

With some good people on board, I expanded the launch day idea that focused on the pizzas and other products. To drive sales, we set up what I called a best display contest for bakery and deli managers, with prizes like a TV or microwave oven. Capitalizing on opportunities to create and push awareness of our product is what it was all about, so what better way to do this than by marketing our product on Super Bowl Sunday; one of the days that the most amount of pizza is consumed.

We set up huge displays and hired part-time workers to conduct demonstrations for four to six hours. Like with the models in the beer tasting events, the temps were paid on a commission basis for pizzas sold.

The demonstrations were such a success that we ran the same thing for Thanksgiving. I was told that I was crazy, but I knew that people must get tired of eating turkey. With this in mind, our advertising signs read: "Eat a pizza—save a turkey!" and we sold thousands of them. Sometimes you have to plant the idea in people's minds for them to recognize it's what they want.

I was in that role for two years, and in the first year we took the region from a couple of hundred thousand dollars to just under a million. In year two, when we had three major supermarket chains and numerous smaller food businesses on board, we made almost three million dollars. All the hard work and continuous effort, helped greatly by surrounding myself with knowledgeable people, started to pay off. Like me, my team was not afraid of hard work and grasped the opportunities I'd painted for them.

Key learning points for this chapter:

- ❖ Don't be afraid to take on new challenges. Sticking with what you know will eventually limit opportunities.
- ❖ When recruiting, you have to sell yourself as much as you sell your company.
- ❖ Don't always rely on your traditional markets. Branch out into new territories whenever you can and always look for bigger opportunities with greater volume and potential.
- ❖ Get your customers to 'love you to death'—the best in sales comes from the best in customer relationships.
- ❖ Don't be afraid of failed sales. With every 'no' you are one step closer to a 'yes'.
- ❖ Good leaders always lead by example, and in times of need, they're never afraid to get involved and roll their sleeves up.
- ❖ When recruiting, see the situation from the candidate's point of view. You need to sell the job to them as much as they want to sell themselves to you.
- ❖ If it suits your product or service, stay alert to special events where you can leverage increases in sales and build new customer relationships.

Case Study

Background

I worked once with a hospital dietician who wanted to set up her own weight loss center. This was something she'd been longing to do for a while but was nervous about getting started. Eventually, someone suggested that she should get help and recommended her to me.

Approach

The first time we sat down together over coffee I asked her to tell me what she imagined this weight loss center to be. With obvious enthusiasm she began:

"Well, I'll have two to four counselors, a waiting area and ..." and so she went on to lay out the entire 'schematic' of her dream center.

"Okay," I said, "let's now reverse engineer what you just told me. If you want to make your business become a reality, we need to start building all the fundamentals of what that is. So, what are your guiding principles, what is your mission, what is your value proposition?"

She immediately got onto my wavelength.

"I want to teach people how to live a healthy lifestyle without all those gimmicky diets that are out there. I'd tie in that people would not only come to my facility for counseling on what they eat, but they would have the ability to work out with a fitness trainer as well. We'd offer boot camps and the like, too."

With that, we started discussing her need for some affiliations, and I directed her into considering people in her network. She thought that she'd have to do everything on her own but soon realized that she could connect with people she knew, like a cosmetologist. From that, we started drawing a mind map of all her connections.

Having her own gym was expensive, and she didn't have the credentials to become a cosmetologist, but she had her network that she could monetize under her own brand. She would pay a fee for referrals as she built different services into her program, but equally, would receive a fee for people she sent to those offering her 'connected' services.

As Napoleon Hill said, "Whatever your mind can conceive and believe, it can achieve," so we came up with her programs and services, as well as her value proposition and market differential.

I'm making this sound a lot simpler than it was, but I'm sure you get my point. She had all these things in her head but had never sought to draw them all out collectively.

Over the coming weeks, we started to envision what her space would look like and began looking for office buildings and complexes that were in high-traffic areas, with people who might be in her target market. I helped her with space layout and flow, and eventually found her an office and other equipment. Then we did all of the brand and logo work while developing her entire marketing strategy. Within six months she began to get her first clients, and she couldn't have been happier.

Outcome

Today she runs a very successful weight loss business that we are going to start to franchise. She has gone from being a struggling salaried dietician to having real financial independence, but she now understands it takes vision to do that. It also takes courage and conviction because success doesn't happen overnight.

After she opened the doors, she hired a receptionist, then another counselor, and so on—all because she had worked out exactly where she was going. It was in this way that she transformed her dreams into a reality.

6

Fish Where the Fish Are

"The secret of getting ahead is getting started."

Mark Twain

MY NEXT JOB meant I remained in the food industry, but I moved into selling cookies. An executive recruiter contacted me, saying that a manufacturer was looking for somebody to perform mostly the same functions that I had in previous positions: building sales organizations.

This was a family-owned cookie company that had been around for many years. They had independent distributors who sold their products to bakeries and delis in smaller supermarkets and food stores. I knew they wanted my services badly when they offered me an $18,000 pay raise, which was huge for the mid-1980s.

So when I came onboard, I really was the regional manager I had in my title, being responsible for the Southwestern part of the country covering five states. But with that bigger pay check came even bigger problems. On my very first day, I had to fly to Houston to fire the guy I was replacing!

I'd told my boss that he must have been kidding, but no, I had to go tell the guy he didn't have a job anymore because I'd gotten it. After he picked me up at the airport, I told him he was fired, drove him home, and took his company car back to my house. Of course, I felt awful at the time but soon learned that he had been a problem that should have been dealt with much earlier.

He was somewhat lazy, didn't abide by company policies, and never really managed his people; he shouldn't have been hired in the first place. The company just seemed to avoid being confrontational with him, and they were disconnected from the issues happening in their daily operations. As well as hiring me to do a better sales job, I was brought onboard to do their personnel management!

The company was still making good money, but most of that was coming from long-standing relationships; there had been very little growth for years. I think I was the first person ever who truly wanted to do something about their situation, and what started out as issues and problems soon became challenges and opportunities. I certainly knew I'd learn more new skills from this role.

At that time, I had a district manager working for me, and he had many of the salespeople reporting to him. He had a quirky personality but seemed to know his stuff, including how to handle people and distributors. We'd both go out to make sales calls, but it was tough because the company had a very weak independent distributor network that had low profits and high employee turnover.

It was similar to the pizza and pasta company, but the sales representatives had to buy their own white vans and were responsible for paying for their gas with no reimbursement. It got even worse when I learned they also had to pay for their own storage unit and all their own expenses. They had to buy a thousand dollars' worth of cookies and make their profit from the margin of selling the cookies at a wholesale price.

I was in the role for two years, and by the end of that period, 95% of the personnel were different from when I started. But we had a few really good people who stuck it out through tough times, and they started raking in profits once we got things going. The district manager had recruited poor performers and eventually, I ended up replacing him.

After a while, I became a little bit numb to losing people. I hated to see them go because most of them had families, but I had a business to run. I became known as the hatchet man, but that's not what I'm really like at all. I was just doing my job and did always look for possible potential in the underperformers.

There was one particular guy that I kept. He just needed to think outside the box a little more because once he developed a lead, he was great at following through. This man had a quiet demeanor and a soft-sell approach and overall was a very likable guy. He possessed all the right traits and just needed some good business leads. I found him one by sheer accident, and it taught him how to spot a good opportunity from nothing.

We were going around his area together and stopped for lunch at a Chinese buffet. The place was quiet, and after our meal, we spoke to the manager. I told him whom we worked for and asked if he would be interested in putting some of our cookies on his buffet as a dessert. Knowing that a lot of Chinese people like almonds, I mentioned that we had two types of almond cookies. He tried one of each and liked them both.

We sold him two boxes, and a couple of days later he ordered some more. Soon he was buying nine or ten boxes per week. By now my guy had taken on board the idea that other Chinese restaurants would like those almond cookies, and he was selling them into all those places in Dallas. I'd just shown him how to spot opportunities and his follow through brought the company and himself some good money.

I talked to him about the need to understand his target market, and how we were fortunate to have a huge audience to work with. I told him to put himself in the consumer's spot and then fish where the fish are. My job was to go after the big fish, like chain stores, and he had to go out after everybody else.

Once our situation became a little more stable, I was able to put some programs in place with measurable goals and inspection points. I also developed different reports, and one was called a 15-5 report—it took 15 minutes to prepare and 5 minutes for me to read. I still use this today when coaching people.

There was also a high-level Monday-through-Sunday report, which indicated people's work and rest days, plus their areas of focus for that week and the next. Once that was up and running, next came growth targets, which were worked down in detail to exactly how many additional cases needed to be sold each day. Eventually, I got my boss to agree on implementing an incentive plan.

I also wanted to hold some activities to help the salespeople, and the product was ideal for a display competition and promotion. Priced by the pound, we sold cookies in a display unit, from which customers could pick out whatever variety of cookies they wanted. My marketing opportunities were limited, but then I bent the rules and got creative.

I had a two-percent ad allowance that was to be used strictly towards print advertising in a local newspaper, but for me, it seemed much better to spend that money on some promotional prizes that would drive customer involvement and excitement. We gave away TVs and microwave ovens, and we were selling far more cookies than before.

However, the company owner found out about my misuse of the budget. He called me and said he'd heard I'd run a contest. I admitted to that but told him we'd sold a ton of cookies. I won him over after I provided a very detailed financial report showing that using the ad allowance money differently, I could drive more sales through end consumer contests. Thus, the idea caught on, and very soon it was introduced across the whole country. The bottom line was we wanted to sell more cookies, and the edict now was that the two percent had just to be 'used wisely'.

When I started in the role, the region was making around $2.5 million per year, but just after two years, revenues jumped to nearly $10 million.

Key learning points for this chapter:

- ❖ Never wait to deal with issues that can affect your business. Tackle problems head-on and don't try to avoid confrontation.
- ❖ Don't always look to discard the underachiever because there may well be talents that have not yet been realized.
- ❖ Opportunities sometimes come out of the blue. Grasp these with both hands and always look to make the most of what might seem to have limited potential.

- Find ways to understand your best target audience. Fish where the fish are.
- Don't try to overcomplicate your sales and performance monitoring and reporting—focus on what really matters and keep its preparation and analysis as simple as possible.
- Always look for new and different ways to incentivize sales; it doesn't always have to be a direct salary.

Case Study

Background

I had a client that was in the travel business, essentially just a small agency employing about three or four staff. He loved what he did, was very passionate about his company, but told me he wanted to really 'explode' it and get into a lot of different areas besides just traditional travel. He wanted to tap into foreign markets.

Approach

"Are there associations that you can belong to?" I asked at an early meeting. "Are there conferences and conventions that you could attend to help build your credibility?"

"Yeah, I guess there's a lot, but … well … I've never thought about attending those."

"But if you want to make your business known, you need to go where there are other like-minded people. Go where the business potential is and let people know that you exist."

"Okay," he said enthusiastically, "I'll start looking into what's coming up."

"Whoa!" I replied, holding my hands up. "Before you think about that, you need to do some preparation. You need to go there with a plan for who you're targeting, and you need to be able to articulate that what you are going to offer is different and unique, something that sets you apart so you're not just another travel company."

"Yeah, I can see that," he replied after some thought. "I need something that people will remember me by. When I remember folks, it's all about the experience for me, the attention to detail. What I need are customer testimonials."

"You got it! Testimonials are one of the best tools to get business because, in your world, if you are creating a wild experience, your customers will probably tell other people about it."

So, we worked on this, and he arranged to attend his first conference. I also told him to spend his time networking.

"If you want to get into the safari business, network with people that run safaris. Get them to understand who you are and leverage their client base just like they could leverage your client base. Make it a win-win for both parties."

So, he did, and it started to pay initial dividends as we worked on his brand recognition. Meanwhile, he also developed some business partnerships with others in the travel business. One of these was focused on incredibly high-end travel, servicing celebrities and those in the seven to nine million-dollar earners. That's what my client wanted to do.

"But the other guy's already doing that so broaden your horizons and focus on where the upper middle class hangs out," I advised.

"Okay, that's good hunting ground," he said. "So, I guess I need to think about country clubs and higher-end social gatherings."

"Correct," I said. "If you want the high-end six-figure people or even some seven-figure ones you're talking about CEOs and the presidents of companies. So, go to the business owner blogs and those of the CEOs and just observe what people are saying. If you can hook up with some of the people, don't try to sell anything, but make it clear that you can deliver value to them."

He asked me what he could say or do that would deliver value, so I told him he wouldn't know until he got out there.

"You just have to develop what your unique selling proposition is and how you're not just a travel agent. It's about how you can deliver a complete experience that will remain with them for a lifetime."

In a fairly short space of time, he went from being a traditional booking agent, buying airline tickets and booking hotel accommodations, to developing custom excursions for his clients. He started networking with CEOs but didn't try to sell to them. Instead, he offered corporate incentives for rewarding people to drive sales and success in the company. He let people come to him.

That led to his being more of a private excursionist, and now he could hit the upper middle class and start looking after CEOs and Presidents because he also handled their incentive programs

very well. He gained positive visibility with access to high rollers with whom he had established solid working relationships.

Outcome

He now runs three large offices, with clients in several countries as opposed to local operations. He's also continually forging new relationships, attending four or five international conferences each year, and being involved in all the circles his target clients operate in. Most importantly, he has met his goal of providing services to high-earning clientele, positioning his company as a true high-end brand.

7

Don't Be Afraid To Take on the Big Boys

"The starting point of all achievement is desire."

Napoleon Hill

IT WOULD BE another 18 months before I changed roles again, but with mounting confidence in my leadership and creativity abilities in a sales environment, I spent a lot of that time plotting my future. When you understand that your professional skills are growing exponentially, you will definitely want to accomplish more, as I did—I wanted the role of National Sales Manager.

Because of our previous continuous sales successes, my team could now handle our new and existing regional customers, allowing me to go after the bigger national companies. To do this, we had to get the attention of such names as Sam's, Walmart, Target, Kmart, Lowes, and Home Depot. Starting from our region, my team and I wanted to develop national sales positions that would compete with highly recognizable cookie brands. In short, we would take on the big boys by entering their space.

We'd never even been in this type of store before and hadn't attained national presence yet, but when you have a great product, you have good leverage. Beginning with Kmart in Michigan, I called on these much bigger accounts, talking to their merchandising people based in our region. We then called on Sam's and Walmart because they were in the same town, and then moved on to Target as well. They were all national companies, but they had regional buyers and distributors.

After presenting our product, which received good feedback, we offered our prospects the chance to stock it. To sweeten the deal, my people would also manage the distribution and keep their displays stocked. They didn't say yes … yet.

Unseasoned salespeople tend to think that they should only make their pitch once and hope to close the deal; failing that, they walk away and try somewhere else. But if you're aiming to get the big players on your side, you must keep pushing through the "Nos" to get to the "Yes."

After our initial offer was declined, I refused to give up so easily. We would call them until they said "yes," and soon enough, they did. Sam's signed up first, and then Walmart, and the rest followed later. When a potential new distributor learned that we were in the country's largest retailers, it added credibility to our brand.

With these huge stores now in our client list, my team made sure that they were satisfied with our services. However, I still wasn't in a position to get to the national level that I was gunning for. Each company region was run almost autonomously, and while mine was still fairly new and expanding, others were already well established and preoccupied with their existing operations that they almost weren't interested in taking on the major supermarkets.

So, I stuck to my own region for a while longer, developing another innovation that would be rolled out nationally later on—a revision to our pricing strategy. I came to this initially because I believed that our sales could increase materially if we made it easier for our customers to understand our pricing methodology.

We had cookie display with all the varieties and the price was per pound, but often there wasn't even a scale around, so people couldn't check how much they'd be purchasing. The price was set at $1.99 per pound, with the sign stating that it was usually 20-22 cookies in a pound. No one seemed to take any notice, so I decided to change it to $0.99 per dozen.

That approach made our product seem more affordable, and the customers responded very well to this simple and straightforward pricing system. Soon our sales started doubling and even tripling in some of our retailers. We even put up signs saying 'New reduced price' which was technically true.

But all that sales growth in the existing outlets, plus the growth that was starting to come through from the major supermarkets, brought some new challenges for the staff on my team. They were still making around two dollars a case but were now easily moving 400-500 cases a week. Back then this was pretty good money, but they were beginning to hit the limits of what they could handle regarding efficiency, business acumen, and so on.

We had hired most of them initially to push our products on a commission basis, so their skill set tended to mostly reflect their initial wages. It wasn't the volume of merchandise they struggled with, but the prospect of dealing with much bigger people on the merchandising side. It was difficult to root out those who couldn't adapt to their new responsibilities, but we had to protect the volume and quality of business that we had fought so hard to attain.

Another issue was that some of our people were still stuck in the old system, and our discussions on achieving measurable sales and consistent sales cycles had yet to sink in. They were focused on selling the product, but they would only zero in on point A and point B when they also had to consider many other places where they could sell the product between those two points.

They weren't driving volume, maximizing their hours, or reducing their delivery footprint. Some of them were even crisscrossing each other's territory, driving miles between stops to drop off fifteen cases on which they were making 30 dollars. We were already handing them the supermarkets on a plate, yet they still weren't biting.

From a staffing standpoint, as your company grows, you must elevate your employees by setting higher standards for them to meet. It might mean making some replacements, which entails investing in more training and development for those with potential, but you have to bite the bullet. Your staff must be able to roll with whatever changes get thrown your way.

Of course, a higher caliber employee comes with a price, and we had to deliver the compensation that was commensurate with their skills. That, in turn, means the parent organization must give them the right sales tools, from training to marketing materials, to a solid marketing strategy and an excellent product. If you're not willing to provide those, you're just hindering quality staff from maximizing their potential in your business.

After letting some people go, a few of my staff members were truly relieved because playing catch up had become too stressful. Soon we hired good replacements that made an impact at a level of sales volumes where I felt ready to have a conversation with my boss about my future.

My boss was the VP of U.S. Sales but was much happier looking after the day-to-day side of maintaining accounts as opposed to winning new ones. That was my opportunity: he needed a strategist as his right-hand man, and I was ready to fill that role. So, I raised the idea, and he didn't say no, but also, he didn't say yes. Instead, he said he'd think about it!

A week passed, and I reminded him of my success with Sam's and Walmart, saying that we should do it nationally. My focus was on the bigger picture, which was making more and bigger sales because he'd always said to me that a sale 'cures all'. I also reiterated that we needed volume, which would significantly lessen the fires we had to fight. The company always had an approach to growing sales volume from the bottom up but could now implement a top-down scheme more effectively.

There was no telling if all this pushing was going to backfire on me, but I couldn't just sit around and wait for things to happen. When you know you have a good fighting chance for advancement, you have to take things into your own hands and create your own destiny. So, when I finally got the answer, it was almost a bit of an anti-climax.

We were out in my car, and he just casually mentioned in passing that he'd been talking to the owner and he agreed that I should be the national sales guy. The position also included a slightly bigger salary and new goals. That was that, and it was down to me to buy my own Champagne.

But my new position brought exciting challenges, pushing my team further to handle more national supermarket chains. Eventually,

I landed the company's first government contract. Working in collaboration with the Regional Manager who covered the Washington DC area, we secured a deal to put the product into the commissaries on all the U.S. armed forces bases.

This took the company's growth to just under seven percent in two years, and over the next few months I tied the company up with the top three largest merchandisers in the country. All of this was great regarding justifying my pushing for a promotion, but I also informed my boss and the owner about the need to keep consolidating our position by still having contracts with all the smaller, but key outlets on every route.

This change of strategic direction and reverting to building routes came as a surprise to them, but I'd done my homework. On the back of what I'd done, other small suppliers were striking up deals with the major store chains, and I determined that some of the big supermarkets could eventually kick us out. That's what happened.

What I'd learned was that the country's largest retailers were notorious for giving suppliers what was called a 'short runway'. They'd watch things for a couple of years to evaluate the demand for your product and if it went well, they simply figured out how to replicate and sell it under their own label—with almost identical packaging. They didn't bother to notify the supplier, you just discover what's happened when your delivery guy shows up to service their store only to be told that the company is not an authorized vendor anymore.

The fact that they could copy what we'd been selling, right down to the design and coloring of the packaging taught me a big lesson in the need to protect your brand's copyright and trademark. My employers hadn't considered this when first warned, and now they were paying the price for not looking after their intellectual property. Get on people's radar and you become a target. More often than not, people will steal from you if they can, and that includes even the biggest and supposedly most reputable companies.

Fortunately, we had some good years filling up the owner's bank account, and my revised strategy to build trade routes and elevate our presence with the smaller supermarkets paid off. Despite our being taken out of the some of the big stores, we still leveraged old relationships.

Our company was well prepared for speed bumps. I implemented highly measurable sales processes, all of which were subject to consistent and constant review to drive performance since measurement was critical again. Also, our success in creating, managing, and growing new markets brought substantial increases in sales.

As a result of my efforts, the company's bosses asked me to spearhead the North American Operations. We weren't in the biggest stores anymore, but we were most definitely competing well in several given markets. It was in this new role that I learned about the aggression that comes with competing with the big brands—but of course, I was up for a fight.

Key learning points for this chapter:

- Never undersell yourself. Set your goals high because you can't wait around for others to look after you.
- If you want to take on the much bigger competition, then you need to do that in their space.

- ❖ Getting a foot in the door with a bigger company to sell your product can be helped when you look for ways to make it easy for them to do business with you.
- ❖ Trying to get the bigger companies to sell your product often means a 'no' at first—don't give up; be polite but persistent.
- ❖ Design your pricing strategy around your customers and make it as easy as possible for them to understand it. A new and different approach to pricing can mean more sales with bigger margins.
- ❖ If your business grows, you may need a change of personnel who are better equipped to manage demand and understand the sophistication of bigger clients.
- ❖ More competent and experienced staff means a higher cost base so you need to maximize returns—ensure that you have all the right training and processes, and performance measurement tools in place along with the best in marketing support.
- ❖ Don't wait for bigger and better opportunities to come along. Go look for them yourself, and make sure you are at the top of the tree.
- ❖ If you get major stores to stock your product, be very wary. You need an exit strategy if they can easily copy your product and sell it under their own brand.
- ❖ If your product has the potential to be copied, take all possible steps to protect it and your brand.

Case Study

Background

I worked with a technology company, who were not yet a major player in their market, but already had a respectable market

share for their core product; they held exclusive rights to sell the most popular mobile computer tablet.

They were relentless in driving sales and recognized that, to keep their momentum, they would need a radical change in their system. They were earning about $6M annually but wanted to take the business to a different level and knew the tablets were their golden key.

Approach

We started off by hiring new salespeople, but when that process started to slow down because we couldn't find the right candidates, we began to look for independent distributor groups and dealer groups that could help instead.

I went with them to see their existing reseller partners for the tablets and negotiated a better rate for them, setting up a better cost structure. We accelerated their sales plan by putting in dozens of sales representatives, all governed by highly measurable results.

We also did some work on aligning everyone in the company around understanding their role in achieving the overall organizational goals; it wasn't just down to the salespeople. Each member of staff within any company's organizational triangle—from the CEO downwards—must recognize their place, their value, and their responsibilities, and that's what we did with this technology company.

So, with the sales infrastructure in place, and their backup and support fully aligned, we began to focus on some vertical markets that they were ready to build serious business relationships with. The initial targets were schools and businesses in the healthcare arena, the same two classic markets I had pushed the solar panel people into, and the company worked on expanding their share of the wallet as their new strategy began to work extremely well.

"These are areas where you don't sell enough and you're going to lose your exclusive rights," I told the board. "If we don't capture and seize the moment, you're going to get run over by your competitors, and you're going to lose a great revenue stream, a significant portion of your business, and an incredible opportunity."

Part of their strategy to put the company on everyone's radar was to advertise in technology and healthcare magazines, and in educational publications. Predictably, the big boys became upset, and they began doing the same thing. However, they had millions of dollars in their marketing budgets, and my client started losing market share.

They didn't have the bandwidth to attack all the potential markets, but they fought well because the right infrastructure had been set up in the first place. When you take on the big boys, you do attract attention, and when that happens, you threaten their capital.

"It's not going to be long before your competitors are emulating what you're doing in the healthcare space or education space," I told them at the outset, "so let's take this by storm. You can't be all things to all people, and you don't have enough manpower to fight this whole thing commercially, but you can own these two markets for a while and still retain a good share later once everyone sees what you're up to."

Outcome

Today, they still dominate the healthcare and education markets, especially the latter because it is sometimes funded by government entities. Now they're breaking deeper into the government space because their competitors haven't, so the strategy is still working.

Within twelve months, they doubled their sales revenue, and it's still growing. It was the robustness of the strategy that we collaborated on that allowed them to ride out that initial storm where they got the reaction from the big boys. It allowed them to maintain their momentum so their company can keep covering more ground.

8

Marketing Must Be Creative and Different

"Excellence is to do a common thing in an uncommon way."

Booker T. Washington

DESPITE MY NEW and elevated position, my fundamental goals had not really changed. All the areas were already growing year over year, and the tenure of company distributors was at an all-time high. However, we couldn't be complacent, and I was still expected to increase sales and market share by growing the independent distributor base as we expanded into new territories.

One of the first tasks in my new role was to make the revised regional pricing strategy become the national standard. In just a few weeks after that first 'price per dozen' trial in a store in San Antonio, our cookies became their top-selling item. We needed to staff the place with daily eight-hour shifts just to keep the display unit filled as we moved about 400 cases of cookies a day. When I talked to the company owner about expanding that approach everywhere he conservatively, and somewhat reluctantly, agreed with my plans.

Another of my effective initiatives was changing the signage. Originally this was blank so that someone could write by hand the price per pound, but very often it was left blank out of neglect. My study proved that if a price was not specified that people would just walk right by.

I spent some time training people about 'no price = no business' and had some new signs made. The point here is that people won't hunt somebody down to find out how much something is, they will just walk right on by. This is especially the case when, like our cookies, the product is, to a great extent, an impulse purchase.

In today's world, where so much is sold online, you need to find innovative ways to capture people's attention if you want to sell something. That said, specifying value and price still works. It's why products that cost $10.99 or $19.99 are still more attractive than $11 or $20. So, I installed my new price signage back then, and it is still the same today.

You have to make it easy for your customers to conduct business with you. If you look at Amazon, they have truly mastered that concept, and in one or two clicks, you've already selected your product and made your purchase.

The trick is making the transaction so easy that not only does it become a no-brainer for the customer, buying from you actually becomes a habit. If you look at some of the most successful companies, again like Amazon, they keep the process so simple and efficient that people enjoy returning to buy more from them because it's so easy.

After the initial surges came in from purchases with the revised price and better signage, our sales growth steadied, and I spent some time traveling to ensure that all the regional managers had also seamlessly implemented my changes.

One day, I was up in the northeast part of the country where we had very good representation except for one major supermarket chain. At the time, they were the region's market share leader, so it posed quite a hefty challenge for us. My regional manager and I were driving around the area when along one of the freeways a bunch of huge billboards caught my eye.

My marketing budget was still a very frugal two percent, but we needed to adopt new methods of raising product awareness. I found the contact information on who sold the billboard ad spaces, and two companies owned the majority of them. For the rest of our regional visit, my main focus was on how to make the most of those ad spaces on the freeway.

I made some calls to check the general availability and later, my regional manager and I visited one of the two companies. A woman showed us into a spacious room with a large black-and-white map studded with red and green flags; green meant available or available within 30 days, and red meant booked. There were also little buttons next to some of the flags, which signified that the signs were in the parking lot of a supermarket—the exact one we'd failed to crack to stock our cookies.

I leased a number of signs in the supermarket's parking lot for a 30-day trial period, mentioning nothing to my regional manager about my new strategic plan. Our billboard ads depicted huge cookies with the message "available at all these fine grocers…" then listed the four to five biggest stores we *did* have agreements within the area!

The day our signs went up, I had returned to my office from a meeting and there was a voicemail from the president of the 'reluctant' supermarket, requesting urgently for me to call him. I smiled knowing he was probably quite upset that his own store wasn't listed on the billboard advertisements that were on his parking lots, but it wasn't like we hadn't tried many times to earn his business.

He left several more voicemails within the next 24 hours, and the next day I picked up his call, demonstrating utmost patience to strengthen our company's position with this prospect.

Almost from the start, he yelled into the phone, demanding to know how I dared to advertise on the billboards in his parking lot. He ranted a bit more, and then I calmly stated that my management team, my salespeople, and even I, had called on his company numerous times with little to no interest from his people. He abruptly said he did not care about the past, but he would like to see me in his office the next day. It could have been arranged right away, but I told him my schedule was already full, and the earliest I could get in there was eleven days out.

My plan had to work. Those signs cost a lot of advertising money, so I wanted them to be up for the majority of the coming month. To cut the story short, my Regional Manager and I finally secured the business with this major retailer. The company's president also agreed to pay for my billboard advertisement for another 30 days after I agreed to add his supermarket in much larger print.

So not only did the billboards advertise our product for 60 days with 30 free days, I was also able to secure the largest and most influential account in the territory by putting on public market pressure.

Frankly, I initially thought it would just aggravate them; I never thought that a secure business deal would materialize from it, but a light bulb went off when I realized where all the billboards were. Initially, I was just looking at new advertising opportunities, but when they turned out to be located near my largest prospect's parking lots, an edgier marketing approach was needed, at least it was for the very conservative company I worked for.

So thankfully, it didn't blow up on me that badly, but it could've been a lot worse. When he heard about what happened, the owner of our cookie company simply smiled and said, "Is that right?" He was a man of few words, but I think he liked it.

Looking back on that situation, regarding what other business owners might do, you just have to figure out the most creative ways to get business, sometimes pushing the limits. You always must chase your goals and targets, but respectfully. I didn't bash my prospect; the advertisement reflected the truth. Sometimes, what you don't say is what people hear the loudest.

That, of course, brought our company more success, and I learned more about what it meant to have taken on the big boys, the major national brands with their household names. The key point was never to underestimate the power of competition and the lengths that successful companies will go to in order to preserve their market position.

Although our brand wasn't huge and powerful enough to cause a significant shift to our competitor's market position, it was enough for me to realize that a few smart and creative moves could make people look at our entire operation from a different perspective.

Like with many grocery products, the cookie business is very competitive regarding how much shelf space you can get. Companies have to pay for linear footage to get every bit of space they can on the shelves. Normally, there's an introductory fee to get into these stores and it could be $50 a linear foot per store or it could be what's called a slotting allowance of around $20,000 for all their stores. We were starting to displace many of the famous 'traditional' national brands with ours, so business started to materially increase.

But our big competitors had very deep pockets, with ruthlessness to match. So, they upped the ante by paying the stores more money to keep us out. However, our owner didn't seem to care if we lost accounts because he wasn't going to pay the huge fees that many stores now demanded. That part was understandable, but a lot of us had worked very hard to build the momentum we had; now it was all collapsing around us, and nothing could be done about it.

Our increasing brand recognition set us up as targets for major competitors who began to beat us down, but that just wasn't the game our company owner wanted to play. I tried to show him how we could put up a fight, but without backing, the effort was futile. The company is still very much in circulation today with a solid piece of the market, but they don't seem to desire the dominance that I wanted.

Our company's refusal to stand against its competitors caused us to lose business. We were being hammered with slotting allowances and extra promotional fees, essentially all the things we weren't going to do. It felt like we weren't the hard-to-get little gnat anymore, just a big pesky fly that made us too easy to swat.

Since our company was going nowhere, it meant that I already outlived my effectiveness with them. I was just starting to grow and needed some bigger challenges. It was time to move on to seek a new route to the top; even with a huge pay cut.

Key learning points for this chapter:

- ❖ When publicly pricing a product, always ensure that it is clear and easily seen—pricing is your hook, and when no price is shown, people will ignore you.
- ❖ You need to make it easy for customers to do business with you. If you sell online, 'think Amazon' and keep it as simple as possible.
- ❖ Marketing does not need to be extravagant or flashy. Simplicity can be exceedingly effective.
- ❖ Always be on the lookout for different and creative marketing ideas and opportunities. Sometimes it is what you don't say that speaks the loudest.
- ❖ Never underestimate your competition and the lengths they can go to in order to protect their market share and position.

Case Study

Background

A gentleman called one day and said he wanted my help in forming a consulting company.

"You do realize that's what most people who have 'had it' with the corporate world want to do?" I asked.

"Yes, I do. But I know I've got something radically different to offer, and that's what I want your help with," he replied.

Approach

"We are going to have to create a unique selling proposition," I told him when we met for lunch a week later. "How are you going to position yourself, and what will you do that's different that nobody else does? It starts with your brand and what you will ultimately stand for. We need to come up with something creative."

We talked regularly for probably a week and a half, during which he had to work on a business plan detailing what his core products and services were going to be. He had to specify what his network was going to look like, his alliances, people we could leverage, all those elements essential to a business that may affect its chances of success.

He was a very sporty kind of guy, and one day, when we were headed to the parking lot, he started talking about fitness, and that's when it fell into place.

"So what about you ensuring that a business is fit for success?" I asked, stopping him for a moment on the sidewalk. "Ensuring that it's healthy and in good shape—where do people go to for that kind of understanding?"

We started to create a concept of a 'business gymnasium', and while his core competencies were based on some smart ideas around processes and analytics, I suggested that he develop sporting analogies around what he could do about raising

business 'fitness'. Soon the idea moved into targeting a very specific client base.

"How about this?" I asked. "Lots of former sports personalities, when they get past their prime, want some type of business; some might do well by leveraging their brand, but some just don't know how to build a business and they fail."

He started researching sports personalities that entered entrepreneurship, and my assumptions had been right. After developing his marketing materials based on all those analogies, his position evolved into his sweet spot. He now helps fix the ailing enterprises of former sports stars or helps get new businesses off the ground for those recently retired.

Outcome

His business is now four years old, very lucrative, and he doesn't really need those materials anymore since most of his new clients are referrals. He still advertises about a business needing to be fit for growth and success, but his client base is completely different from the corporate audience he once envisioned.

Today, he has also gained the attention of college and high school coaches, so his client base has expanded significantly. They may not be sports professionals themselves, but if they have an interest in running their own businesses, then this guy is the man for them.

9

Do What You Love

"Don't aim for success if you want it; just do what you love and believe in, and it will come naturally."

David Frost

I'VE ALWAYS LIKED building things; it used to be sales divisions, then companies, but most of all, it's people. Whether it's helping someone's personal growth or improving things in their company, it's still ultimately about the central person involved. It feels good to help someone else become a better business owner or a more successful employee.

In the previous chapters, you have read about some of my experiences in helping executives and individuals build their businesses, and there are numerous other people and organizations I've worked with.

Today, my work continues to keep me as active as always. You'll find me constantly on the phone, on Skype, or flying around the world—over 600,000 miles last year—but at the end of the day, it's all about "building a better you," around which I've developed a website, and is also the title of one of my upcoming books.

When my wife suggested that I form a consulting business, it seemed like a great idea and I spoke to my friend and long-time mentor, a guy who had built a personal net worth of over $500M. He confirmed that it was the obvious next move for me. He brought up my momentum that had been built throughout the years and agreed that the time was ripe to strike out on my own.

At the time, I was still working for the non-profit cooperative company, so my personal pet project had to be developed under the radar at first. Eventually, I began getting clients from networking and began building an organization to establish credibility. In turn, this developed into a framework of highly talented people who could support my clients while helping their own personal growth.

Despite my extensive work experience, there was still so much to learn. I attended a business development seminar, which greatly inspired me from being surrounded by so many successful entrepreneurs. The room was full of energy, and the speakers themselves were all entrepreneurs helping others to take their business to the next level.

Altogether there were about 700 attendees, many of whom were in a similar situation as mine; they were currently on somebody else's payroll but had strong inclinations towards entrepreneurship.

My first company, *Momentum Consulting Group Inc.*, is an organization with a well-rounded set of disciplines that could be taken to the international marketplace. Learning again from my past and harnessing people, processes, and products, I wanted to serve our clients in the areas of sales optimization, training and development, data analytics, supply chain management, process improvement, and sustainability.

Along the journey, I also met aspiring individual entrepreneurs who needed the foundational understanding to start a business or conquer a plateau. So, a separate company called *i-Consulting Group* was formed to focus on individual attainment versus the corporate infrastructure design or sales acceleration that we were doing through *Momentum Consulting Group Inc.*

Starting *i-Consulting Group* required a business model that helped new and aspiring entrepreneurs and executives garner the knowledge they need, coaching them from an outside perspective, and helping them tap into their greatest potential for their chosen field. Even the name *i-Consulting* speaks for itself— 'I' being about personal and not necessarily corporate consulting. Today, *i-Consulting Group* operates under the Momentum umbrella.

Both companies have clients touching six continents in over 38 countries worldwide. We act as mentors and strategists, working on implementing best business practices that can be deployed in an organization, and help develop executive-level strategies for the top corporate executives wanting an external, unbiased opinion on themselves and their business.

I greatly enjoy conducting individual consultations. The challenge is both exciting and gratifying, bringing grassroots help to address fundamental business concerns. It also takes me back to the times where my skills, character, and businesses were tested and fortified over the years. Let me share with you another example of a past project.

One of my clients in Europe is a guy whose company built highly interactive top-end websites. This was a distinctly competitive market, and he still needed more people, but he was a horrible manager. His lack of management skills resulted in constant employee turnover and several thousand dollars a month in losses. Together, we evaluated and targeted his key issues in depth, and within a year and a half, the developed solutions shot his annual revenue up to almost $20M.

One of the simplest things he did was to employ a skilled manager, so he could focus on the creative aspect of the job, which he excelled at. I also worked in the same way with a doctor who needed to turn around a failing practice because he was trying to be a business manager, which was not his forte. Again, his poor management skills put him in severe, almost crippling debt.

I said to him, "With all due respect, management is not your strength. I'm not a doctor; you're not seeing me practice medicine. Focus on what you're good at."

As well as concentrating on his medical acumen, he specifically needed to focus on becoming a long-term family physician to younger patients since his current ones were older and would eventually pass away.

To that end, we created marketing campaigns and strategies targeted at the younger generation, resulting in a thriving practice. He went from nearly being bankrupt, and conducting more lectures than seeing patients, to providing consultations to a steadily growing stream of paying patients.

At first, it was a bit intimidating to provide consultations to lawyers and doctors, directing them in how to run their business. It wasn't easy to candidly let them know that they were not good in certain areas. At times, it felt like being a psychologist and business coach all at once. Understandably, it's also difficult for them to share their failures and weaknesses and want to be corrected. But real growth begins with identifying your biggest issues and strengths, your best skills, what motivates you the most, and what you love doing.

My approach to reshaping and redirecting my clients towards success is by helping them focus more on their talents rather than their weaknesses. It's a given that we're all flawed in some way. There are a lot of things I'm not good at, and there's no point wasting precious time focusing on them. Instead, I get talented people to perform these tasks, while I apply my best efforts using my particular skill set. That's always been my approach, and it should be the case with anyone who wants to be successful.

Recently, I worked with a lawyer who was struggling for relevance in a highly competitive market because she was too focused on small clients. She needed to redirect her focus towards bigger clients if she wanted to build a stronger career.

She mentioned a big bank that was about to release a major bid, but there was no way she could compete with the more powerful law firms. When I asked her, "Why not?" she said she didn't have the manpower. But she affirmed that she could find a way to get it. I advised her to envision herself in the future, which she did, and ultimately won the bid.

It was the same as when we submitted the bid for the big public-sector job worth over $500M. On top of careful planning and strategizing, I had everyone work as if the account was already ours, and we acted from a future-based perspective. Doing this puts you in a frame of mind that's much more aligned with your target's mindset and goals.

It's an often-used phrase, but business owners also need to think about working *on* their business and not *in* their business. If you have all the people who have the expertise and skills to deliver your product or service, you can work on business development.

Very often, successful business owners are their own brand ambassadors. They're practically living advertisements for their enterprise. That's what I tell people to do: go out, deliver value, and the money will come.

So, the question you need to ask yourself is this: "What's your unique selling proposition—your personal USP?"

This should be divided into two things—telling people what you do and telling them how they can benefit from what you do. My job is about helping that USP come to life, it's about building people up, building their lives, building their knowledge base and credentials. That's how I got started on this path in the first place.

Someone asked me what the most common thing is I say to my clients now. The answer is, "99% of people give up when they're just inches away from greatness." You just have to persevere, to believe in your abilities, and maintain your conviction about what you're doing.

Be careful about naysayers who don't have your best interests at heart; sometimes they're your competition, and sometimes they can be your closest friends or family members. I'm very fortunate that my wife is extremely supportive of my pursuits because she knows it's what I love.

I tell people not to give up, and quoted Napoleon Hill before, but Thomas Edison also said, "Our greatest weakness lies in giving up. The most certain way to succeed is always to try just one more time."

Looking back at the first seminar I attended when I was thinking of going out on my own, the highly successful people there all spoke about perseverance. It takes just one person, one deal, and one opportunity to change your life. You should never, ever give up, and you must have a relentless desire to succeed. As I quoted at the start of Chapter 2, Milton Berle used to say, "If opportunity doesn't knock, build a door." If you can dream it, then you can achieve it.

You must be willing to change and adapt, to adjust your perspective when needed and, most importantly, you must listen. Thinking outside the box is difficult when you're in it; you can't see the picture when you're the picture frame. That's why people need coaches, to help them look at their concerns from a different angle, and to help them grow.

Doing what you love and focusing on delivering value is what I so strongly believe in. But don't forget to sell yourself as well—people buy from people first, then companies.

I continue to build my business on relationship capital, one referral after another. As Barry Finlay, the Canadian author who climbed Kilimanjaro at age 60 said, "Every mountain top is within reach if you just keep climbing."

Key learning points for this chapter:

- ❖ If you are moving into self-employment for the first time, you must accept that, no matter how successful you were in your previous career, there will be things you do not know.
- ❖ If you're not the best at managing people, employ someone who is and focus on your talents.

- ❖ Throw off what you see as your current limitations—think beyond today and imagine yourself in the future.
- ❖ As much as possible work *on* your business and not *in* your business. Aim to have other people around to deliver today so that you can think about tomorrow's business development.
- ❖ Make sure you—and everyone else necessary—understand your unique selling proposition. Tell people exactly what you do and show how you can benefit them.
- ❖ No matter what setbacks you might experience, always believe in yourself and have conviction in what you are doing.
- ❖ You need to be willing to adapt, change, and look at things differently—when it's time for you to consider it, seek outside help.
- ❖ Do what you love and focus on delivering true value; again, remember that people buy from people first.

Case Study

I thought it would be appropriate to close with a story about my friend Dean Cardinale, who's been a huge inspiration to me. Dean owns a company called, World Wide Trekking, an adventure tour guide company, and I first met him in mid-2015 when I hired him to guide me to the top of Mount Kilimanjaro. This was the hardest thing I've ever done in my life, but it was also one of the most unbelievably fulfilling.

Upon meeting Dean for the first time, we actually didn't immediately get on the topic of our upcoming climb but rather talked about business. When I asked him what business he saw himself in, travel or trekking wasn't his response. Astutely, he described himself as being in the customer *experience* business.

For Dean, creating memories that last a lifetime is just as important as guiding his clients safely on their adventures. Ensuring his guests have a world-class experience that will live with them forever is what he conscientiously strives for on each trip. This conversation continued throughout our time together, and as we eventually made our way back down the mountain, I remember bringing up his attentive staff and how they made all of us feel so special.

If more companies understood the concept of creating a memorable experience for their customers, they could be so much more successful. Dean's genuine passion for his clients' experience ultimately rubbed off on his staff. Dean, in essence, was leading by example.

Dean's belief is that meticulously and competently guiding his clients up Mount Kilimanjaro, Mount Everest, Machu Picchu, or any of his other adventures, is his life's mission. When you treat what you do for a living as your ultimate purpose in life, that kind of love is palpable. For Dean, it shows through his words and actions, and in the way he motivates people when they are struggling during the roughest and toughest moments of a climb.

It was an amazing trip but, of course, it was unimaginably hard for all of us in the group who had never experienced such a thing before. Climbing Mount Kilimanjaro taught me a lot of good life lessons, ones that required more inner strength and faith than I thought possible.

Every single step you take to get nearer the summit of Mount Kilimanjaro is a huge feat. With the lack of oxygen at such high altitudes, your body simply wants to give out. Step. Stop.

Breathe. Step. Stop. Breathe. That's how it was for hours and hours as we moved at a snail's pace in our quest to reach the top.

The way Dean encouraged and motivated us not to give up was to have us repeat to ourselves "Success, success, success" with every step we took. When we talked about this after our descent, we agreed that this applied to any business, too.

Just like climbing a mountain, success in business is also about taking one step at a time. Start saying to yourself, "Success, success, success" after each step you take to move your business forward. Keep putting one foot in front of the other, realizing that with each set back you're still getting closer to your targeted goal.

For the final ascent, we set off at 11 p.m. and climbed all night. When we finally reached the top at seven in the morning, the sense of achievement was overwhelming because the climb was especially difficult on that last glacier.

"Think about your family and friends who are counting on you to do this and think about that one small step," Dean said as we set out. "Don't look up. Just keep looking in front of you."

And that's true in business. Don't look at the mountain you've got to climb but look at the next step you've got to take. Remember that, at one point, you're going to be at the top of that mountain—it's the momentum effect that will keep you going.

Momentum Consulting Group has delivered over $7 billion in sales to businesses across six continents in 38 countries. They are regarded as a global leader in building powerful national sales organizations by offering a complete range of business-enhancing solutions to elevate companies and organizations striving to achieve their goals and objectives.

Momentum Consulting Group will guide you to imagine your potential and create the strategy that will allow you to experience your vision. Momentum will help identify your strengths, weaknesses, and goals, both for the short term and the long term. They will then take that strategy to increase sales, boost profits, expand your reach, and open the door to new opportunities and market dominance.

Understanding that your organization needs to improve is one thing; knowing precisely how to make those changes in a practical and efficient and pragmatic manner takes well-developed strategies and years of expertise. **Momentum Consulting Group Inc.** has all of that and more, and their strategists will help you gain the momentum you need to thrive. They know the types of challenges and obstacles you face as you strive to grow and expand. They have the solutions.

Visit: www. MomentumConsultingGrp.com
or call 800—764—1875

To succeed in today's highly competitive global economy, you need to understand if your business is following the right strategy, and whether your sales, marketing, and online opportunities are being optimized. A fresh pair of eyes ensures that you are putting your efforts into the aspects that will lead your business in the right direction.

From a personal perspective, whether you are a business owner or a rising executive, everything is built from relationships. Maximizing the value in those relationships is critical. A mentor can help you take your business or career to the next level and elevate your brand and income.

I-Consulting Group has done all those things, they've been coached by the best and have worked at the highest levels. Now they want to share their years of experience so that you too can achieve the success you have always yearned for beyond your wildest imagination.

Visit: www. MomentumConsultingGrp.com
or call 800—764—1875

CPSIA information can be obtained
at www.ICGtesting.com
Printed in the USA
BVHW052139090523
663902BV00012B/314